In loving memory of my wife
Barbara Beattie Howard née Walford
1936-2020

Acknowledgements

I could not have put this book together containing letters from my Army service from Sept 1947 to 1949 had it not been for the efforts, or even need, of my late mother to keep those letters and must give her my special thanks for having handed them to my family before she passed away in 1963.

I am also grateful to my son and daughter, Mark and Sue, and their families, who have shown an interest in this part of my life and given me the encouragement to put it all together.

I particularly thank my son, Mark, for encouraging me to make arrangements for the letters to be published in this book.

Many of my handwritten letters were carefully typed by Lucy Caswell, for which I am very grateful.

I must also thank Roy Williams of Leighton Buzzard for his continual encouragement and advice, particularly with regard to the 'introduction' to this book.

I must also remember those friends who wrote to me in Egypt (details of which have been lost over the course of time) as well as my occasional tent colleagues and visitors who I can remember; notably Dick Bradley, Peter Bains, and others including Jack Hewitt, and Johnny O'Neil who may also be in my photos.

It was mentioned that as we were short of clerks we received some WRAC office additional staff which I recall included Mary Hodge, Mary Stewart and Sally Peters who gave so much additional office support until Mary Stewart and Sally Peters were, I think, allowed leave to get married. One of these colleagues was transferred down from Palestine with very interesting stories of her adventures in Jerusalem.

And so this all went together to make my nearly two years Army Service in Egypt an interesting and worthwhile experience, even adventurous, that created the need to put all my letters into book form, even at this late date. The reader may appreciate that these letters were written by an Englishman having, *inter alia*, so much content about the weather, naturally being part of our 'upbringing' in England.

Preamble

Perhaps I might use the traditional phrase of "Who do your think you are" to try to explain a brief history and analysis of my life as far as I can remember.

I was born in a small end-terraced house in Wallasey on 11th January 1929, the first-born to a couple who had lived through very difficult circumstances in their own lives and had married a year earlier in an effort to look forward to a better life which they felt was available to them.

So Kathleen (née Grant) married David Edward Howard and went on to have three children. I was the eldest, with a younger brother, Keith Grant, and then Patricia Marjorie, both of whom married and had families, as did I.

Sadly, both Pat and Keith have since "passed away", but I am fortunate to remain in touch with their families.

But I shall concentrate on my own life which I recall as a child was somewhat adventurous – being free to wander with local friends in the local parks and being close to the promenade and beach as well as the sandhills at Harrison Drive. The promenade was an ideal place for me to enjoy travelling on my roller skates with friends.

Everything changed on 3rd September 1939. I was in our back yard when there was knocking at the communal entry gate. My mother came out of the scullery and opened the gate to receive some news from a neighbour who lived opposite. Turning to me with a serious, even severe expression, she announced "The War has started".

I would hear "grown-ups" talking about various happenings which would be reported on the wireless on the BBC Home Service and in the newspapers.

Gradually, we began to notice searchlights being positioned, barrage balloons and gun emplacements. As we were on the coast, we also saw triangular concrete blocks and minefields being positioned near Harrison Drive to protect against invasion. Dare we throw stones into the minefield? Perhaps not!

In Green Lane and not far from our house, anti-aircraft guns were put into emplacements and eventually the army began to practice. Now things were getting exciting as, of course, my friends and I would walk to the gun-site to watch. Occasionally a barrage balloon would come down in flames and soldiers would walk past us with their rifles.

Soon, rationing was fully operational. I was often sent to the shops with our ration books and a list of things to buy. I felt we never seemed to go short although this was because our parents would be very careful. I remember the ration books to this day.

But we would carry on with our usual lives, attending school, going to the cinema, ("the pictures") on Saturday afternoons. Outside school hours we would play our games in the park and go to the seaside at Harrison Drive which was close by. Like most young boys we enjoyed catching tadpoles and other small fish which we kept in jam jars. Unfortunately, they never seemed to survive very long.

We accepted our gas masks without question and we carried them in their little box everywhere.

On the night of 12th March 1941, air-raid wardens came and advised us to proceed to the communal shelter in Granville Terrace. Only minutes after I was taken from my bed, an incendiary bomb smashed through the roof and burst into flames on my bed. I remember being in the shelter vividly; hearing the terrifying bang of an exploding land mine, and the chaos that ensued.

After the "all clear" we emerged to see rubble everywhere. We crunched our way through slates and broken glass back to our own house which was uninhabitable. It was thanks to the air-raid wardens and to my mother that I survived.

Nevertheless, I made sure that I was able to rescue my Meccano Set Four, which became my favourite "possession" at that time.

After we were bombed out, we were rehoused in Prospect Vale, Wallasey. I adapted quickly to the changes that were taking place because, as a young boy, fear and excitement went hand in hand. At least we had not been evacuated; on reflection I was glad we stayed at home to experience what to me were real 'adventures.'

After air-raids, finding shrapnel was an essential activity. We compared collections and "trophies" with school friends. The pride of my collection would have been an unexploded (live) incendiary bomb which I found in an EWS tank in Prospect Vale. Sadly, I was not allowed to keep it… in fact it created quite a commotion when I took it home and showed it to my father. I could not understand what all the fuss was about!

Finding pieces of Cordite was also a novelty. Together with my friends we would (as all boys do) share our knowledge of these things and cordite was another dangerous commodity which we would together put into a jam-jar, drop in a lighted match, put a brick on top, and run. The ensuing "bang!" was hugely exciting.

Then, there was a mine washed up on Harrison Drive beach with its probes sticking out quite clearly. Whatever our boyhood darings were, we knew that this was something we should keep well clear of.

There have been other memorable experiences which I need to recall. One of which was waking up to a cry from my mother who found me covered in spots from measles, an infection so severe that it caused permanent damage to the eyesight of my left eye.

I remember a somwehat happier moment when I was advised that I had passed the Scholarship to the local Grammar School.

We took holidays in Garnedd Fawr farm in North Wales where I enjoyed playing with the local farm boys who were keen to show me their way of life, including how to ride horses 'bareback".

I also enjoyed talking to the farm milkmaid, who would invite me to drink milk direct from the teat of the cows (via her milking tube). I remember enjoying that so well.

They were also keen to teach me some of their own local Welsh language so that in due course I was eventually able to sing "All through the night" in Welsh with my local madrigal group.

And I recall clearly the outside open lavatory at the back of the farm with the wooden seat; we must remember that there was no central heating in those days. But we survived…

The 'Secret'

Whilst in Egypt I received a letter from my mother explaining that she was in touch with a 'cousin' Raymond (Ray) Grant in the USA, enclosing a letter from Ray to my sister, Pat, and suggesting I should also write to him. With the regret of hindsight, I did not.

What I did not know at that time was that Ray was not a cousin at all, but was in fact my older half-brother, born to my mother in 1920, some years before she met my father.

This only came to light in 2017, following a family history DNA test taken by my son, Mark. By coincidence, Ray Junior, Raymond's son, had also taken a DNA test. There was a match; my mother, Kathleen, was their shared grandmother.

We learned that in 1926, at the age of six, Ray was put in the care of a Catholic "orphanage" in Birkenhead. This should probably be understood in the context of the complex familial, social and religious sensitivities of the time.

In 1936, the time came for Ray to leave and so he went to serve on a cargo ship on the North Atlantic trade, eventually settling in New Jersey, USA. He remained in contact with our mother.

Ray became a US citizen and started his own family. Although he sadly passed away in 1993, before we knew the truth, and before I could meet him, we are now happily in touch with his family, thanks to the wonders of DNA technology.

While it is regrettable that all this was not known earlier, it gives me a better understanding of what must have been a cause of deep regret for my mother, who would surely be relieved and pleased to know that the truth is finally out, and that it is OK.

I like to say, "to forget is easy, to remember is a challenge". I hope that such memories will remain in my family as well as my life through these "Letters from Egypt" that she held on to.

Preface

Perhaps this is the story of the one who had to go away although not in the way one would have wished! (To forget is easy – to remember is a challenge). However, at the age of 18 after leaving school it was an interesting time for adventure, and a time for travel. Perhaps a time to see what the world has to offer.

It was in September 1947 that the letter dropped on the mat. It was in a brown envelope marked "OHMS" or "On His Majesty's Service".

I looked at my mother's face, I remember a mixture of stern but worried expression of anticipation and expectation. A sense of change seemed to overcome her as she opened the envelope. Inside was a rail ticket and Government instructions, not for her, but for her eldest son, now 18 years of age, requiring him to proceed on 18th September from Seacombe station in Wallasey to Chester Northgate station where I would be met by a contingent of Military personnel and police and to be taken with others by lorry to "The Dale" Army Primary Training camp at Chester.

Of course, these young men mainly of around 18 years of age are just one batch of British young men who have just left school and who have literally been taken from their homes by decree of King and Government to do National Service and to keep the peace at various British strongholds at home and overseas after the end of the war.

Such a drain on the youth of our country must conversely seem strange to the older generation left behind just as it did during the war where conscription and bombing and evacuation took its toll.

My own National Service was eventually spent in Egypt and the story of life in Egypt during that two years has been preserved in my many letters home, most of which I still have.

Through these letters, I can recall most of my adventures after leaving home; Primary Training in Chester with the Cheshire Regiment, learning discipline, how to behave properly in front of the drill sergeant, out on the Sealand firing ranges with the Lee Enfield .303 rifles and Bren guns. But also the discipline of making one's bed, how to roll up shirt sleeves, polishing boots and gaiters, even how to adjust your beret.

Then marching in the parade ground, how to salute when passing an officer holding the King's commission (who would be required to salute back).

The basic training would normally change you from being an ordinary young man, probably in his teens, to a soldier ready to defend his country.

After some leave we were required to report to the Training Centre at Blackdown, near Aldershot, all recounted in the postbag, to be trained for overseas duties, although we did not realize this at the time, learning army codes, document formats, despatch methods, telegraph systems, how to type, and so on.

At Blackdown Camp we were billeted in buildings with room areas each taking about 20 soldiers to sleep on metal beds, albeit reasonably comfortable. Our further training was to take about six weeks although some of us, after tests, were "passed out" before the end of the six week period and sent on leave, which happened to be over Christmas 1947.

After completion of this leave (for which we were eternally grateful) and return to Blackdown, we were transported to a transit camp at Thetford in Norfolk to await "disposal".

Conditions at the Thetford transit camp were not pleasant and how long this would go on for we did not know but it could be a week or two or even longer. Perhaps it was designed that way to make us look forward to going to a permanent overseas posting. whether it be the Far East; Middle East; Europe; Germany, but anything would be better than Thetford. At that time, I did not have the courage to report the details of the unpleasant conditions to my mother in my letters.

This was not a happy situation but we were allowed an hour or two to settle down by our beds and then required to proceed to the mess room with our tin cans; tin mugs; and tin knives and forks. So we queued up for our meals and each found a table to eat from along with our other newly arrived young "soldiers".

The following day we had to assemble outside in rows where we hoped for movement instructions. But no, the sergeant came around and asked whether anyone knew anything about "weights". This, I thought, would be to choose a few men who might have reasonable knowledge of mathematics and therefore be clever enough for some particular posting and to be transferred out of this awful place. So, I volunteered, something I have since learned "not to do".

But, in fact, the question was raised to choose a few men to act actually as "waiters" in the officer's mess. This was quite a shock. Not only was I not being shipped overseas in the short term but being given boring work which could go on.

The main advantage of such "temporary" boring work was that after the officers had finished their meals we had no shortage of food and there were some comfy chairs in which to relax.

It was at this point that I wished that I had accepted the offer to go for Officer training and wrote the following extract from a letter home:

> "The Americans condemned the camp a few times, then the RAF moved out, and we are still here even though it is condemned. I think the best sound I have heard in this camp was last night when the postmen called "Howard 878" two letters!
>
> Well tomorrow I will know my fate. If my name is on the notice board for draft posting, I'll be alright. But if it is not, goodness only knows what will happen. I think I would apply for a home posting…"

But, in fact, the next day I was able to write:

> "I am going abroad after all, I was posted to 11 Platoon yesterday evening, and we are due to sail next Tuesday on the OTRANTO from Southampton.
>
> As you will see we are a week overdue and if we don't get out of here soon something is going to happen. Soldiers are being brought back every day after deserting.
>
> Well I'm afraid I'm too fed up to write any more. In any case there isn't anything to write about except that I haven't received a letter from you for a good time."

And so it was that our orders came up on the notice board and after waiting at the officers mess for a good two weeks we were detailed for draft DEGNT, to assemble with full kit for transport, first by army trucks to the railway station at Thetford and then by special steam-train (of course) around London to Southampton.

I must admit to being somewhat impressed by the organisation that took us in one hop from a small country town, around the Metropolis and then on to the quay at Southampton, so that when we got off the train we found ourselves at the foot of the gangway leading up to what appeared to be an enormous passenger vessel which had in fact been requisitioned and converted to troopship RMS OTRANTO at the outbreak of WWII.

We eventually found ourselves on a messdeck with hammocks and still no news as to our destination. It seems that the Authorities were not prepared to take any risks over "losing" servicemen on the way, as in the extract from the following letter:

> "Anyway, later the same day, the vessel singled up and we left the quayside with tugs fore and aft to proceed slowly down Southampton Water and around the Isle of Wight to the open sea, destination unknown. I felt the first roll of the vessel as we proceeded out to sea, past the Isle of Wight but we did not have to wait long after sailing before news came that we were destined for Port Said, Egypt, with calls at Gibraltar, Malta, Pireaus and Salonica with further destination Singapore via the Suez Canal. This caused great excitement and some sadness as some of my friends found themselves destined for Singapore. For some strange reason I had no appreciation of how my parents might be feeling without any news or knowledge of where I was or how I was progressing.

> There was no feeling of homesickness as I found my eighteen years at the seaside kept my senses at full stretch as the new experience of voyaging into the open sea was completely new and even exciting. We were now free to roam along the open deck and take in the ozone also to watch the waves go by and the seagulls as they followed the ship. Until we entered the Bay of Biscay!"

It was January 1948 and cold. The Bay of Biscay was at its worst and living up to its reputation. So along came my first spell of seasickness and even now I can recall the dreadful nausea, probably made worse by the knowledge that it would be a further two days before we would be in the calm waters of Gibraltar harbour.

But it passed and even now, memory after memory of the "cruise" keeps coming back. The passing of Cape St. Vincent, the arrival in Gibraltar Harbour, gazing in awe at the Rock, where I was able to post a letter to mention about views of Cape St. Vincent and views of the Rock. The voyage was becoming interesting but otherwise nothing much to report, weather getting warmer, nothing much to do. Perhaps my mother would be pleased at my better news?

At Malta, we anchored in Grand Harbour, Valetta along with the Mediterranean fleet. Nobody left and nobody came, a bit like in the poem "Adlestrop" by Edward Thomas, but I did not know that poem at the time. Otherwise much of the same, reporting flying fish, dolphins, and porpoises, leaping and flying along with the ship. Still nothing much to do except read, write, even chat, probably unusual for the male of the species.

Next port Pireaus and then Salonika, the second largest city in Greece, passing Mount Olympus northbound, the highest mountain in Greece and the home of twelve Olympian Gods. Our voyage was becoming very interesting.

Otranto; passing the Rock of Gibraltar; local Arab vendor's boat at Port Said harbour

We discharged arms and ammunition at Salonika, out in the harbour, to help the war effort of the Greeks against the Communist revolutionaries in the hills only a few miles away. It is probably fortunate that my parents were not aware that I was in a war zone at the time.

The voyage from Salonika to Port Said, passing Mount Olympus southbound and between the Green Islands of Greece along the Aegean Sea. It was then that our geography lessons were suddenly coming alive, with an appreciation of our geography master, "Spud Widlake", who will live forever in our memoirs.

At that point we learnt that some of us were to disembark at Port Said, and others to remain on board to Singapore. This did create some excitement as we had learnt about Egypt only in school books.

And so I think it best if I should recount briefly some of my adventures which in many ways have been a shock to the system.

First of all on arrival at Port Said and in the harbour many small Arab boats came alongside trying to sell all sorts of commodities, but these were just a fascination. We gingerly descended the ship's ladder with full kit weighing a ton into a landing craft, being careful not to fall into the water, and reassembled in the barge looking back and up with wonder at the OTRANTO, and on berthing alongside the landing stage we were to step foot on Egyptian soil.

At that point we were surrounded by very important looking and efficient Military Police in white webbing and with revolvers in their holsters directing us from the quayside direct into a large lecture hall.

There was no way out and no way back and so in the hall we were subjected to a fascinating lecture by a senior officer on what we would find out about life in Egypt, the dangers, behaviour, and survival procedures. Also what to do, and what not to do in Egypt.

The first thing we were to do was to put our documents and valuables into our inner pockets. All in all we were given a picture of a den of vice; of thieves who would use every trick to steal your belongings and valuables and more importantly how they would do it, and of 'Ladies' who would appear friendly and leave you with a sickness that you would regret for the rest of your life.

Films were shown about looking out for the tricks used by thieves; the diseases and parasites that would hit you by drinking local water or putting your hand in the Sweetwater Canal. The Sweetwater Canal was known to carry every known disease and if a British or German soldier as much as puts a finger in it he has to receive 37 injections at the British Military Hospital at Kabrit. No punches were pulled and the advice given we were to learn was not overstated. It was in many ways fascinating to learn something so different to our teachings of Reading, Writing, and Arithmetic, or the rules of Rugby. How different to our understanding of social behaviour and trust as we knew it in England.

The lecture subsequently proved to be very timely as on leaving the lecture I found a local with his hand in my pocket – but he got nothing!

And so, after our introduction to a different world we were marched to a railway siding for embarkation onto a special Egyptian State Railways train for the 100 mile journey to the Base Transit Depot at Suez. This journey can be recounted from my letter dated 10th February as follows:

> "On the 90 mile journey to Suez which took five hours I saw more sights in a day than I have ever seen before in one go.
>
> Starting at Port Said, with a horrible grounding sound, the train pulled out of the junction. There was no platform and the train was made completely of wood, the seats were like those in Harrison Park, there were no windows (glass I mean). Instead of windows there were venetian blinds.

Every time we stopped we were waylaid by Egyptian vendors, selling tangerines, handbags, bananas, watches, rings, jewellery etc.

We have been issued with Egyptian currency, and in exchange for £2 Sterling, I got 200 Piastres.

In this camp, nothing is rationed, everyone gets 50 cigarettes at 2/6d (12 piastres). Of course I will get them and exchange them (100 for a watch, which is a good one), or sell them at increased price to heavy smokers.

Oranges are ha'penny each, sweets and chocolates as much as you want. Films developed in 24 hours at one and tuppence. Everything is sold by Egyptians employed by the British.

They are typical of the pictures, long white flowing white robes, with a sash, a turban, bare feet, or a piece of cardboard for sandals. We saw thousands of camels on the way down, and palm trees and native mud huts in the Sahara Desert on the way alongside the Canal."

But being in transit gave us a chance to become acclimatised and another new experience happened after arriving at the Base Transit Depot as found in the following extract:

"At the moment we are having a bit of a sandstorm, and the tent is swaying, of course, we hope it stays up. The sandstorm got quite bad this afternoon and almost blew our tent away. All the sides were almost being carried off, and all the other tents' main parts had been ripped off and vanished. We were the luckiest but even so there was sand over everything. I got my eyeshields out and used them. Four of us out of the thirteen occupants of the tent strove to keep the tent standing and intact, and after some hard work we got it slowly into shape in the terrific wind, and made it fairly windproof."

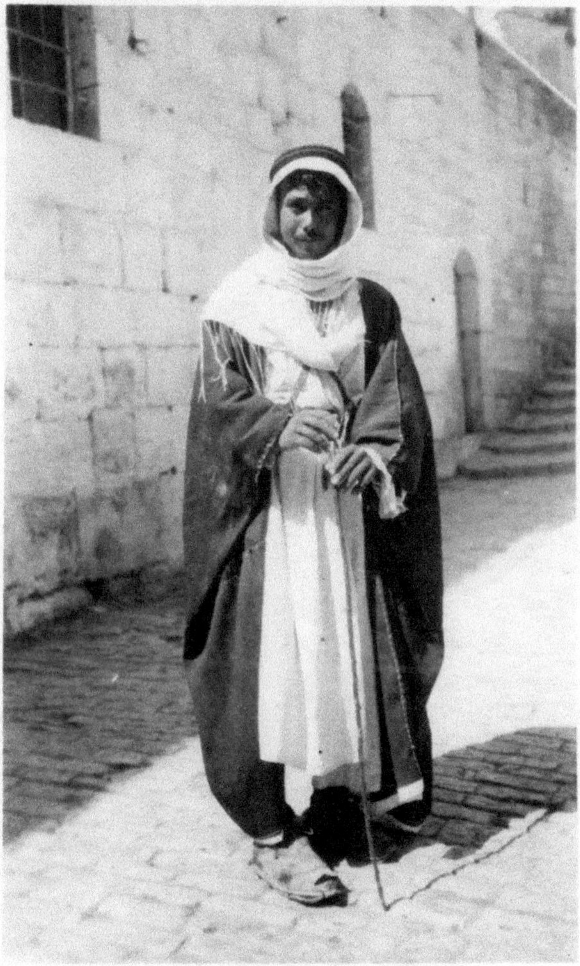

But we were young and in our own way fascinated by the initial experiences which stood us in good stead in the years to come.

After Transit camp we were moved for duty with the Royal Army Service Corps (or RASC) to the Headquarters of the Middle East Land Forces at Fayid at the side of the Great Bitter Lake on the Suez Canal but also we were camped by the village of Fayid, occupied by local Arabs and a fascination for British servicemen. We found that there was a mix with local tradesmen and shopkeepers allowed by the British authorities. Because of the heat of Egypt, working hours were adjusted to take this into account and swimming in the Bitter Lake was encouraged. The Lido controlled by the British Authorities was a great attraction to British Troops in the area and food was plentiful compared to rationing at Home.

On arrival at the GHQ Army camp we were directed by the Corporal to a tent in which there were six iron-framed beds with wire springs and a paliasse. On enquiring as to when we would be moved to permanent accommodation the answer came back, almost apologetically, "Oh no, son, this is your home for the next couple of years".We looked at each other in horror but at the age of 18 you are flexible and can accept such situations quite quickly.

And so, we flung our kit-bags onto our beds and looked at our 'furnished' accomodation to see how this could be improved. First of all a few pictures cut out of Picture Post to hang on the walls of the tent. My first picture was a photo of a thatched cottage in the village of Cuddingtion, near Exeter, my friends also had some pictures, some a bit more 'risque'.

Our tent measured about 18 feet square and I managed to get into one of the four corner positions. After introductions we lay on our beds to consider the future. Two years living in a tent, working in GHQ Middle East Land Forces, but on the positive side two years in the hot sun and swimming in the Great Bitter lake only a mile away during our time off. We did not consider how our parents felt.

As far as I can remember my 'friends' in the tent were from various places in the Country which gave a beautiful variation of accents which made life interesting. I know that I managed to acquire a cupboard probably from somebody going on demob and so my furnished accommodation was complete. I don't think I had explained all this to my parents in my letters?

And so it was, after settling in and meeting our other tent "newcomers" we had to get used to our environment and after getting to know our workplace we then got together and decided to study the "Village". We found that we were able to walk from our camps through the village and over a bridge crossing the Sweetwater Canal (which was usually full of dead animals floating on the surface) and we would pass "Jock Macgregor's" occupied by a local shopkeeper trying his best at a Scottish accent. Also fascinating was Khan Kalil displaying a fully wrapped "Mummy", or other shops where the owners tried to entice "rich" soldiers inside.

At the far end of the village was our Lido alongside the Lake which was very welcome and necessary for a two years stay of duty in Egypt and perhaps a bit like the French Riviera.

But whatever impression I might have given with regard to periods still to go before release, I must say that on reflection I can now appreciate the benefit of my experience of the twenty-one months National Service in Egypt and the pleasant adventures we had at places like the Seaview Holiday Camp at Port Fouad, of the Derby Day Fete at Fayid, my many days at the Lido, the Beach, and warm waters of the Great Bitter Lake, with the hot sun contributing to these days. (It may be curious to note that the continual comment in my letters about the weather as we found it in Egypt can only come from someone brought up in Britain where the weather is a way of life).

I will always remember the young Arab who came to me outside our office crying in pain with a nail in his foot and asking for help. I held him firmly, got his foot, the sole of which was like leather, and pulled at the nail slowly but gently until I had got it out for which he was so relieved and so grateful.

I was also able to visit the Holiday camp at Lake Timsa, Ismailia, and the town itself crowded with interesting people speaking different languages. A group of us were also able to cross the Great Bitter Lake in a launch on an adventure to explore the edge of the Sinai Peninsular. I must also mention the superb entertainment that was constantly available (out of office hours, of course), in the Cameronia cinema, Music at the Fayid education centre, Library, Concert Hall, as well as competitive games.

I must also quote the following letters written at different times which to me bring back interesting memories, such as the Fete Day in April 1948:

> "At the moment the Basutos[1] have just entered to entertain us with some music. They are in a special type of Army Dress with Bush Hats. The weather is terrific, there are some white cotton-wool clouds about, the sun is warm, and there is a nice cool breeze. As for the scenery, at the far end of the field is a grove of Palm trees. On the left is the Lido Club (a modern type of building).
>
> Three Basutos have now got into a type of march and have started with the drums like a tattoo. There is a drum Major, a massive African swinging a stick, and dressed in a red sash across his chest. The leading four drummers are dressed in leopard skins. They are a fine example of the British African Army. I forgot to mention, they have all got red, white, blue, and yellow tassles and have white ropes dangling from the drums."

---

1 Basutos = People from *Basutoland*, a British Crown colony that existed from 1884 to 1966 in present-day Lesotho.

Port Fouad; Sinai; Gebel Shawbrit; Basuto parade at Derby Day Fete

In January 1949, an unforgettable concert:

"Last night we went to the GHQ theatre to see Ivy Benson and her All-Girls Band. I can easily say it is the best show I have seen in my life, and I wouldn't have missed it for anything. With the band were the O'Hara sisters (The Maids of Swing), like the Andrew Sisters, then there was Joan?, singer and comedienne, and also Gracie Cole, the best girl trumpeter in Britain.

The drummer is an 18 year old girl from Liverpool, and the xylophone solo was also by a girl from Liverpool. There were a couple of monologues by a girl with a wide Lancashire accent who also acted the fool once or twice in the band. The band consists of 15 girls and Ivy Benson. The whole thing lasted two hours and we got to bed at midnight."

On 27th April 1949, a potential attack foiled:

"In Cairo the police have found three big secret arms dumps, which they think were going to be used for terrorist activities. The biggest in 22 Docki Street, Shubra, Cairo contained 400 Hand Grenades, 1000 sticks of gelignite, eight machine guns, four vickers Guns, two Sten Guns, 18 Tommy Guns, eight fruit baskets filled with sticks of explosives and cordite, Molotov Bombs, large quantities of Gunpowder, millions of cartridges and a workshop. But Cairo has been saved."

And on 13th July 1949, when I felt in a descriptive mood:

"On Saturday night we went into Port Said and passing along the Boulevard Fouad 1[er] we saw a cabaret just starting, so we went in to see what it was like. There was a cover charge of 12.5 piastres. Inside it was the usual night club style and at 11-o-clock a floor show started… at 12 midnight the Belly Dancing started, and carried on till 1am when we all bailed out. I got to bed at 2 am."

My letters have created a magic of reminiscence that brings back such an infinite variety of memories and made it appear as if it were yesterday. I must therefore give special thanks to my mother for keeping my letters, and to my friends in Egypt (details of who have been lost over the course of time), but also to those friends in England and elsewhere who did write to me.

Dave Howard
August 2022

The Letters

27th January 1948
At Cambridge

Dear Mum and Dad,

Very many thanks for your registered letter which I received safely last night.

At the moment we are travelling straight through to Southampton. When we leave tonight we call in at Malta and disembark at Port Said, from where we are posted. We had 15 lorries to take us to Thetford Station. We left Thetford at noon and are due to arrive at Southampton at 7pm. We are travelling in a first class coach. I keep on gazing out of the window and half dozing off as on Sunday night I was on guard and we had to get up at 4.30am this morning. Yesterday was the most hectic day I have known so you can guess how tired I should be.

You will probably be thinking what the matter is with my writing, well it is just the train which has a peculiar habit of swaying and going up and down. The atmosphere in this carriage is not what you would you would imagine it to be. All is quiet as the majority of us are devoting time to a more useful purpose than the usual sing-song. There are over 400 travelling on this train.

We have just stopped at Bishop's Stortford – started again – travelling through fairly dull country. When it gets dark I will be able to put the small lamps above my head on, it's got a flashy shade. At the moment I have got the ideal feeling of comfort, slightly different to being at Knettishall Camp (damn the train).

The time is 1.45pm and we are still in dullish country – the train is stopping – a hundred yards away is/was a terrific mansion house surounded by a lawn – very flat country – big patches of water everywhere – just passed through Cheshunt – Waltham Abbey – Enfield – Angel Road – Tottenham – Lea Bridge. There are some massive junctions in this region. Passing through Stratford and tube terminus – also the burnt-out skeleton of the massive Carnico confectionery works – passing Victoria Park and Austin's motor works – Hackney, Canonbury, Highbury, Camden Town, Kentish Town, Gospel Oak, Hampstead Heath, Finchley Road, West End Lane – (just gone completely across North and Central London) – Kensal Rise, Willesden Junction, Kennington North – and Clapham Junction (Southern Railway). I think only special trains are allowed to do what this train has done, namely, to cross from the LNER line in East Anglia right over to the main Waterloo – Southampton Railway.

It is getting dark now and everyone sounds very happy the further away we get from Thetford. I will have to wait until I get to Port Said before I can get the film developed now, so I will send you the photos instead of the film.

In another one and a half months I will be getting 7/-[2] per week more and I will then be a 1-star private and if I am lucky, I may be a L/Cpl[3] or a Cpl.

I suppose we will be issued with the foreign money when we get there, and the climate will be nice and warm and help to practice singing. It is going to be terrific. All the great singers come from such a climate.

Well, Mum and Dad, it seems as if it is all for now, but you can be sure that I will write again as soon as possible which will probably be a couple of weeks, as naturally I won't be able to write from the ship. I have heard it is a good ship.

Give my love to Keith and Pat.

All my love,
David

---

2 /- = shilling
3 L/Cpl = Lance Corporal

10th February 1948
No.5 (RASC) Rft. Coy.
Draft DEGNT
Base Transit Depot,
M.E.L.F. Egypt[4]

Dear Mum and Dad,

At last we have arrived at the transit camp. It is situated in the semi-desert region a few miles above Suez at the end of the Suez Canal, and is quite a decent place although it is very big.

OTRANTO arrived in Port Said at 6pm last night (Monday 9th Feb). We disembarked at 7am this morning and got aboard a very primitive train by the quayside at the beginning of the Suez Canal (Egyptian State Railways).

On the 90 mile journey to Suez which took five hours I saw more sights in a day than I have ever seen before in one go.

Starting at Port Said, with a horrible grounding sound, the train pulled out of the junction. There was no platform and the train was made completely of wood, the seats were like those in Harrison Park, there were no windows (glass I mean). Instead of windows there were venetian blinds.

Every time we stopped we were waylaid by native Egyptian vendors, selling tangerines, handbags, bananas, watches, rings, jewellery etc.

We have been issued with Egyptian currency, and in exchange for £2 Sterling, I got 200 Piastres.

In this camp, nothing is rationed, everyone gets 50 cigarettes at 2/6d[5] (12 piastres).

---
4 M.E.L.F. = Middle East Land Forces
5 2/6d = 2 shillings and sixpence, expressed as "two and six" [sixpence = half a shilling]

Of course I will get them and exchange them (100 for a watch, which is a good one), or sell them at increased price to heavy smokers.

Oranges are ha'penny each, sweets and chocolates as much as you want. Films developed in 24 hours at $^1/_2$d. Everything is sold by Egyptians employed by the British.

They are typical of the pictures, long white flowing white robes, with a sash, a turban, bare feet, or a piece of cardboard for sandals. We saw thousands of camels on the way down, and palm trees and native mud huts in the Sahara Desert on the way alongside the Canal.

Tonight the weather is clear and warm, with the white dust of the scrublands hard beneath the feet. Towards dark we could see the silhouette of the African mountains outlined against a bright red sky.

I hope you will write quickly as we will probably be here only ten days, letters take three days by airmail so you can try and get one here before I leave. Don't forget to send it by Forces AirMail, and it will probably be 6d.

Much love to all,
David

12th February 1948
AG1((b) Branch
GHQ
M.E.L.F.

Dear Mum and Dad

I hope you are receiving my letters alright. I shall be expecting one from you about next Monday 1st March. Letters usually take about three days each way.

If you have not received my letter from GHQ I will repeat that the address shown above is the only address. If you put 'Egypt' on it takes two weeks to arrive and I have been told that you should not put 'Fayid', even though that is where we are.

At the moment I am in the information room at the Education centre, there are all sorts of activities here. Photography, cycling, wireless, music, swing club, tennis, hockey, skating etc, etc.

I have had the other films developed (the first one in Wallasey), but in some of them I have not got the idea of the speeds. But I will soon get used to them. Every film on the third reel was good and clear.

On the first reel the decent ones are
- Looking west from St. Hilary's tower
- Looking North from St. Hilary's tower
- Looking East from St. Hilary's Tower
- Deepcut Village, Hants.

The darkish ones (over exposed a bit) but details visible are:
- Express on Southern Electric Rly (Waterloo – Southampton)
- Me in Bishopsgate, London EC.
- Alan Simms in Bishopsgate, London EC
- A wooded road in Hampshire

- M.C., J.W. and J.L. on Harrison Drive
- Muggy Wray and Keith in background (Harrison Drive)
- View across the golf links (from Harrison Drive)

Spoilt by overexposure:
- Don Sauvage's vain effort to save a kick from Keith in Harrison Drive.

Absolutely spoilt
- Keith kicking a ball.

I have just read in the papers that Britain is in a cold spell and that snow has fallen all over the country. It seems strange to hear such news as at the moment our temperature is 75°F and we are also in a cold spell. In summer it is cool to have a temperature of 100°F, but hot if it reaches 130°F which it often does.

The sun has been out continually since we arrived in the Port Said region. The weather may be called similar to the British mid-summer (in a hot spell).

I see New Brighton drew 2-2 with Southport, also that Everton won and Liverpool lost to Middlesbro'.

My friend Bill in the office comes from New Ferry, Birkenhead, so we often talk about familiar things. He recognizes Claremount Road from St. Hilary's Church Tower.

Well mum that seems to be all for now, I hope to be receiving my first letter from you soon. Don't forget my address.

Much love to all,
David

18th February 1948
AG1(b) Branch
GHQ
M.E.L.F.

Dear Mum and Dad,

At last the time has come. I have been posted to General Headquarters of the Middle East Land Forces at Fayid in Egypt. I am working in the Filing and Registration Office of the Adjutant General No. 1 Branch, GHQ, M.E.L.F, Fayid (at one time GHQ Cairo) is the same as the War Office in London.

It is probably one of the best postings I could possibly get at my stage, being a beginner. I really feel as if I have started halfway up the ladder and I like it. I never thought conditions like this could possibly exist in the British Army.

We arrived at Fayid railway station at 8.15am after getting up at 3am. From there 21 of us came here, about 15 went to 2nd Echelon, GHQ, and others were posted to different companies of the Royal Army Service Corps (RASC) in this district.

Another good thing about GHQ is there are representatives of every Corps and Regiment in the British Army, all mixed and working together. Also it is terrific company. At first in all the transit camps everyone used to swear, smoke, and drink like blazes, but I had no effort to keep myself apart from these individuals.

Now, however, everyone is of a refined breeding and I hardly ever hear a swear word. Naturally almost everyone smokes, but not to the extent of these drivers and storemen in transit camps. I don't think anyone drinks to any extent.

Everyone calls me by my Christian name and they are all willing to help me with any difficulty. When I had to carry a heavy bed from the stores they all fussed around and took off me and fixed it up for me.

The office is clean and has a fan in the ceiling, there is a sort of servant who does odd jobs. Although I do not do any typing there are two typewriters in the office not being used.

In the office there is a staff-sergeant whose name is Don (we all call each other by our Christian names), there are two sergeants, one lance corporal, and one private plus me. For promotion you have to be a Class 2 Clerk (I am Class 3). To be a Class 2 clerk there are exams, which, I have heard, are pretty easy.

There is plenty of entertainment, there is a shopping centre and a civilian quarter (whites). There is a married families quarter and Auxiliary Territorial Service (ATS) quarter and a school.

The railway runs through the middle of GHQ and roads in GHQ itself (where I work) are terrific. Main avenue has four carriageways, (keep to the right) and has grass 'islands' all down the centre, the wide pavement is palm tree lined.

There is everything you can wish for (except a gramophone, wireless, or piano in the tent). Later in the year we will get Khaki drill (KD) and mosquito nets.

Every minute of the day locals come round with baskets of fruit, books, chocolate, newspapers et.etc. The cookhouse is 50 yards away, the lavatories are 50 yards away, and the washhouse is 50 yards away. Laundry takes 24 hours, there are plenty of films, cameras, watches, fountain pens etc., cheaper than in England.

The shopping and civvy town centre is a few yards away, the NAAFI's[6] not far. There is a roller skating rink and 'Grand' ballroom and restaurant in the shopping centre. All the shops there are clean and modern, the roads are wide. All the shops have verandas with armchairs, tables, and cool drinks on them.

Here in the office we deal with Top Secret, Secret, Confidential, and Restricted letters, it is one of the most important parts of

---

6   NAAFI = Navy, Army and Air Force Institutes recreational establishment

GHQ. I had to sign a form before I came in to say that I would keep all secret information to myself.

To get into the GHQ compound I have to have a pass, and this had to be shown at the gates before I come in.

Two yards away is Major Grice, he is the DAAG, or Deputy Assistant Adjutant General as at the War Office. The Grades are:

- Chief of the Imperial General Staff (Monty)
- CIGS (Monty again)
- Adjutant General QM General
- Ast Adjutant General AQMG
- DAQMG
- Deputy Asst AG (Major Grice)

This is at the three main offices of London (War Office), Fayid (GHQ M.E.L.F.), and Singapoire (GHQ FARELF).

The hours here are from 8.15am till 1.15pm and on Wednesday, Monday, and Friday from 5pm till 8pm.

In Summer we go down to the beach for a swim and a rest in the hotel there. There is no reveille, I get up at 7am or 7.15 am.

We have decent billets and beds with three white sheets and three blankets. We can construct any furniture, we are given an iron locker which is as safe as houses. Ours is a cosy place.

Well I had better send this letter now, but first I will say do not put 'Egypt' on a letter as it will take two weeks to arrive. Just put my address like this:

S/21041878 Pte Howard J.D.
AG1(b) Branch
GHQ
M.E.L.F.

Much love to all,
David

5th *March 1948*
AG1((b) Branch
GHQ
M.E.L.F.

Dear Mum and Dad

If you haven't received my previous letter, I should like to say again many thanks for your two letters.

We are having some hard days' work lately as the Chief Clerk, Don Ranson is in dock with a growth in his right shoulder. So now two clerks of AG1(b) have got to do all the work that comes in ourselves and get it out again. We just manage to do it and keep it going. This is really how the offices work.

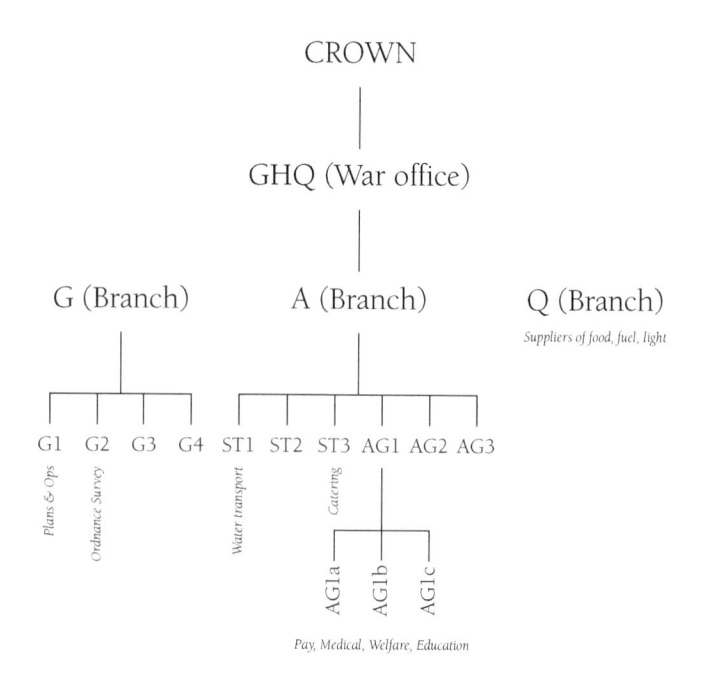

```
                            CROWN
                              |
                       GHQ (War office)
                              |
    G (Branch)           A (Branch)            Q (Branch)
                                            Suppliers of food, fuel, light
   ┌──┬──┬──┐      ┌────┬────┬────┬────┬────┐
   G1 G2 G3 G4    ST1  ST2  ST3  AG1  AG2  AG3
   │  │          │         │         │
 Plans & Ops  Ordnance Survey  Water transport  Catering
                                      ┌───┬───┐
                                     AG1a AG1b AG1c
```

Pay, Medical, Welfare, Education

Of course it goes down and down such that we control many different branches below us. Our work is mainly administration and if we make a blunder, something goes bang.

On Tuesday I am going to see a film on the Olympic games of 1936 in Berlin. At the moment our sports are being held before the heat of summer comes, it is just like the school sports except that we have a sand track.

The bloke next to me, Jim Veal, who was in Cairo with GHQ said he has seen the pyramids and sphinx at Giza. Cairo is 90 miles away.

I have just run out of sweets so I went and got another 1lb[7] tin of butterscotch. All the chocolate and sweets I get are made in Britain and they are not rationed. I don't know if I have told you before, but absolutely nothing whatever is rationed out here. Some blokes who have been here a couple of years give a faraway look when you say the word 'ration' and they will suddenly say "Ah yes! Isn't that what they have in England, it must be rotten."

By the way, mum, could you get that snap of "A Highland Herd" enlarged to a decent size and then send me the negative. The object of you getting it enlarged is so that if the negative should get lost in the post I will have the benefit of the photo at least. Also could you send some newspapers, please.

I could also do with a Spanish book and a map of Africa. Of course it will all take time, but that can be expected.

For some queer reason the weather has gone cool for the last two days, but I suppose it will go hot again soon. March, however, is the coldest month out here.

---

7   1lb = 1 pound imperial weight [454 grammes]

Here is a sum for you:

٢٣١٥٨   Answer: ٨٦١٧٦
٩٦٧٨
٥٣٣٤.
―――――

The numbers are, of course, in Arabic.

١ = 1
٢ = 2
٣ = 3
٤ = 4
٥ = 5
٦ = 6
٧ = 7
٨ = 8
٩ = 9
١٠ = 10

Aywa = yes
le = no
Ala kéfik = it doesn't matter anyway you want (?)
Imshé = scram

    Don't forget to keep on writing. I hope to have a letter tomorrow.

Much love to all,
David

P.S. *Mail goes from GHQ airfield to Nottingham and then to Wallasey. Similarly, mail goes from Wallasey to the A.P.O in Nottingham, and from the army airfield there to GHQ M.E.L.F. and straight to us one mile away. TIME = 2-3 days*

March 1948
AG1(b) Branch
GHQ
M.E.L.F.

Dear Mum and Dad

Many thanks for your letter which I received on Monday. Everything is going smoothly here, I am going to save a bit from now on so that I can get a good pair of curvy worsted trousers which are abundant round here, also I may get a good stop-watch for £1-10-0, I want to save £6 by July so as to go to Cairo-Luxor-Thebes on a town, still I am not sure what arrangements have got to be made yet.

I have finished off another roll of film. As soon as I get the chance I will send home all my snaps and some negatives.

The weather is still keeping just right, not too hot, and not too cold. A couple of days ago we had a slight bit of rain and I went and stood in it just as I was, it felt terrific.

What is my poor old bike like now that Keith has finished with it. The poor thing must be in pieces by now.

Don't forget to send a white shirt, a Spanish book, and some music. I hear that we are allowed to send clothes home if they have been worn and classed as personal effects, so when I get some money and you are short of any type of clothing, I can buy some, wear it a bit and then send it home, But, don't be anxious and send British money because it is a crime to have it in this non-sterling area. Perhaps it is possible to exchange British for Egyptian in a Liverpool foreign exchange, but we'll see about that later on perhaps.

- 1 Egyptian Pound = £1 sterling
- 100 piastres = £1 and £1 Egyptian

- 10 piastres = 1/-
- 1 piastre = 2½ d

    I haven't got Dad's letter with me but I think he said that Keith had fallen over again. Well, anyhow that can't be helped can it? But I am glad to hear everyone is keeping normally fit in the British condition.
    It is time to knock off work now so I will hope for another letter tomorrow.

With love to all,
David

March 1948
AG1(b) Branch
GHQ
M.E.L.F.

Dear Mum and Dad,

Many thanks for the parcel containing shirt, films, books and music. Also a parcel of newspapers, and also a separate letter from Dad, and one from Mum.

The parcel containing the films got through the customs alright although it had been opened at one end (the end opposite the films).

I saw all about the choir and Maunders "Olivet to Calvary". Ole Ted Mellor is there again, bashing away at the top notes I expect.

I have just been down to the NAAFI and played all the music, but I'm afraid the piano is getting rather antiquated.

This afternoon I played monopoly, there were six of us altogether, and of course, I won. I ended up by owning all the board, except Oxford Street, Regent Street, and Bond Street.

As I am writing this letter I am eating more sweets, I have had dinner at 6.30pm and a supper which is a repeat of the dinner at 7.15pm

For a pudden we usually have prunes and custard, or bananas and custard with cream. The tent is full of empty ice-cream cartons at the moment.

Yesterday I did a bit of removing, I moved over to AG1(a)'s side of the room to help them out as the chief clerk of AG1(a) has gone on demob and left the place quite empty. So seeing as the chief clerk AG1 thought I was capable of doing AG1(a)'s work until a new clerk arrives he put me on it and left AG1(b) to fight for themselves.

We are all in the same room, however, and we all know each other so that letter addressed to AG1(b) will arrive just the same. You can put AG1(a) Branch if you like, but it doesn't matter as whichever person goes to Registry to collect the mail gets all mail for AG1(a) and AG1(b). In AG1(b) there is:

- Chief Clerk:Sgt Ginger Scott who comes from Lambeth.
- Clerk: L/Cpl Dillon who comes from Wolverhampton; (formerly of New Ferry, Birkenhead).

In AG1(a) there is:

- Chief Clerk: Cpl. Brummall (Brummy) who comes from Wolverhapmpton
- Clerk: Pte Allan, who comes from Perth, Scotland, and
- Me

I have got to learn Chief Clerk's job as well as my own as quickly as possible because they think I am the only person who may be able to take the place of Brummy when he goes in June.

Well seeing as a couple of blokes are in bed I may as well…

Much love to all,
David

7th March 48
AG1(b) Branch
GHQ
M.E.L.F.

Dear Mum and Dad.

I have just received Monty's letter from you. I will write as soon as possible and send him one as soon as possible.

I want to say something about pay as I have been in the army now six months and am entitled to "1 Star" or 1/- per day extra. When I came in the army pay was 28/- but I only drew 27/- so that 1/- per week was going in credit.

When I came overseas I got an extra 6d per day (or 3/6d per week) put in credits for being here. That means 4/6d per week is going in credits. Now that I have one star, I get an extra 1/- per day, but as I do not draw that 1/- per week yet, it will all mount up in credits.

So I draw £1 per week, allotment of 1/- per week, credits of 11/6d per week from now onwards.

In about three months time the one star will come into effect and I will draw the 7/- per week extra if I want but don't forget that the back pay for the one star is all in credit.

Everyone is talking about demob here and it is always the general conversation morning, noon, and night. One bloke wants to take seven suits home, one for every day of the week, any chance they get here is to go into civvies[8] and get down to the beach for a swim in the Blue Lagoon. In a conference in GHQ a question came up and it may mean that we will be able to wear civvies for work.

---

8   Civvies = civilian clothing

The date for going into KD[9] has been changed to 1st April as the weather is still only like the British summer. I haven't been issued with KD or a mosquito net yet.

In Monty's letter he says he has been posted seven miles north of Brunswick, anyway I will send his letter so that you can read it, when I have finished with it.

Last night I saw the film "Spellbound" with Ingrid Bergman and Gregory Peck. It was quite a good film.

We are going to play Monopoly now so I will finish hoping that conditions at home are improving.

Much love to all,
David

---

9 KD = Khaki Drill [uniform worn in hot weather]

8th March 48
AG1(b) Branch
GHQ
M.E.L.F.

Dear Mum and Dad

First, many thanks for Keith's and Dad's letter. As soon as I saw the first part of Keith's, I knew what agony was to come, I'm afraid I was laughing my head off for a good half hour until they put the fans on to cool me down.

So ole Froggie's retiring eh? I suppose the Boss will give an exaggerated speech which will probably start, "This term we we are losing a very good friend in Mr. Bohs. His devotion to his work and teaching was invaluable and he was respected at all times by his pupils…" etc.

There seems to be a bad turn with Pat, don't forget to write often and let me know how the old arm is getting on.

I'm surprised at Keith for almost forgetting that Liverpool beat Huddersfield by 4-0 instead of 4-5. Blackpool and Manchester United are the two teams I forecast for the Cup, three weeks ago.

Yesterday (Saturday) I went to Ismailia. It is a terrific place, and being esentially a French town, it is built on French lines. The majority of the population are French and Spanish, all the notices are in French and there are some in German such as, "*Halt reben der strasse*" and "*Rauchen Verboten*".

There is a terrific park there which is abundant with green vegetation, grass lawns, date palms, coconut palms, tennis courts, hockey and football pitches and a promenade where it meets the lake and the Canal.

Across the lake we could see the massive Australian War Memorial. We also saw the foundation stone of Ismailia inscribed all in French (of course). I had to translate everything for the two blokes I was with.

The centre of the town has terrifically ultra modern shops, the place was crowded with people of all colours and nationalities from Sudanese to British families. They have the latest Chrysler, Buick, and Studebaker cars from America. Converging on the centre of the town are tree-lined four-lane avenues with terrific European residences on either side.

I went into a modern store and passed someone being served, they were talking French. A bit further along someone else was being served, they were talking Spanish.

There was all the latest of clothing, watches, handbags, suitcases, and nylon stockings by the million. And nothing is rationed.

The two best clubs in town are the YMCA and the "Blue Kettle". They have palm-fringed verandas and balconies so that you can bask in the heat of the tropical sun 'And so we return from this land of dreams and vivid colours, deep canyons and sombre gaeity'.

I got to bed at 12 am. Some of the gang were playing Monopoly (aye, we bought one) on my bed, the cheek of the working class. This morning I got up for breakfast at 9am and went to church afterwards.

After dinner we went on a "safari" up to the mountains with a particular desire to get to the top of the nearest and biggest. Four of us went on this trek and I finished a whole roll of film on the way up. As we approached the mountains from the scrub-desert it was just like being in Texas on the films (cowboy), white trails and sand backed by queer rock formations. When we got amongst some rocks we started playing Cowboys and Indians!

It was very interesting from the Geographical and Geological point of view as there were many different types of Igneous rock as well as fossils and animals bones. The region is volcanic, and near the top we came across white volcanic ash.

On the top we could see for many miles across ridge after ridge of hills until they merged into the proper Sahara Desert. The other way we could see right across the Bitter Lake and Deserts of Sinai and on the other side which also includes Sodom (The Bible).

This region is inhabited by stationery tribes of natives who build their villages in valleys. We saw one of these.

One person in our office (an ATS), who has just come down from the King David Hotel, Jerusalem has got a lot of snaps taken in Jerusalem and Bethlehem. There are all the gates including Damascus Gate, views of the centre of Jerusalem, views in the Temple, the Church of the Nativity, which has terrific carvings in the roof and walls and some of the finest windows in the World as has the "Church of all Nations". She showed me photographs of all these. Also there were many views in the Garden of Gethsemane.

We have a POW German orchestra playing once a week here in GHQ, and I missed a programme of music by Bach and Handel. I have decided to go to the theatre this Christmas to see a Pantomime.

Next week (middle of March), we go into KD as the weather is too warm for walking out dress which we wear all the time.

The Bishop of Egypt is taking a confirmation in Moascar Cathedral (six miles away) on Thursday.

On my first leave I am going to a free holiday camp at Port Said where you get waited on hand and foot and where there is everything you can think of to do. On the next leave which comes soon after, I am getting a free travelling warrant and going on a tour of Cairo, Luxor, and Thebes in the Upper Nile around Aswan, which is in the Sudan.

Well that is all for now. Hoping to hear tomorrow.

Much love to all,
David

PS. Please send the two films. I will try and send some French magazines for Keith (from Ismailia).

11th March 48
AG1(b) Branch
GHQ
M.E.L.F.

Dear Mum and Dad,

This letter will probably be a continuation of the one I sent this morning. I've got 4.3/4 hours off before going back at 5 o clock.

Most of the fresh news is mainly from the papers. First, the temperature at Giza, Cairo, early last Monday morning was 32°F, and everyone is shivering here, the locals say it is the coldest they have ever known it, yet I feel quite warm and so do all the others who have just arrived. Naturally the temperature during the day here, is much warmer than 32°F, it often touches 70°F, but it shows that the diurnal range of temperature is quite a lot.

The car of Lieut-General GHA Macmillan, Commander in chief of British Forces in Palestine, was blown up by an electric mine on the Jaffa-Jerusalem Road, day before yesterday. The General was not in the car. You will probably have read about it in the British Papers.

I have just heard that the First Division are to send a team on a short visit to the Canal Zone. They are going to play three games, the second of the three will be played at the Great Bitter Lake Stadium, GHQ Fayid, on 21st March.

The finals of the GHQ athletic meeting and inter-branch Championships, took place on Sat. 28th Feb at the new Fayid Stadium. General Sir John T. Crocker KCB KBE DSO MC, C-in-C M.E.L.F. gave the prizes. Here are the times:
- 100 yards Major Lockwood 10.4 Secs
- 220 yards Major Lockwood 23.8 secs
- 440 yards Major Philip 56.8 secs

- 880 yards Capt. Buist 2mins 11.3 secs
- 1 mile Sgt Green 5mins 3.2 secs
- 3 miles L/Cpl Speight 17mins 28.5 secs
- 120 yards hurdles Major Manners 18 secs
- 2 mile walk L/Cpl Williams 18mins 1.6 secs
- High Jump Lt. Marshall 5ft 4ins
- Long Jump Major Lockwood. 20ft 7ins
- Pole Vault Major Manners 8ft 3ins
- Hop/step/jump Lieut Marshall 39ft 4.5 ins
- Putting the weight 2/Lt Trafford 34ft 2.5 ins
- Throwing the discus Major Manners 105ft
- Javelin L/Cpl Maugham 154ft
- Hammer Capt. Stone 77ft 6.5ins
- 1 mile relay 4 mins 21.3 secs

Tell Keith to send me some comments on these.

Last night I saw Deanna Durbin in "I'll Be Yours" and it is one of the best American films I have seen for a long time.

We are getting stacks of work in the office, so much that I don't get time to see if there is any more gen on demob. I will be glad when Don comes out of hospital.

Well mum, I think I will wait now until I get a letter from you.

Much love to all,
David

12th March 1948
AG1(b) Branch
GHQ
M.E.L.F.

Dear Mum and Dad

Many thanks for Dad's letter which I received the day before yesterday. You seem to be having a mixture of bad luck and good luck at home, tell Keith not to worry about the School Cert as the need for a good rest is more important and there is plenty of time. It is quite an easy exam and he knows enough to get it now.

It is only a week after the Grand National, and already I have seen photographs in the London Times of the race, we are not far behind England with news etc.

The Rector sent me a short and friendly letter, saying how it was a great pleasure to receive my letter, and went on to give a summary of he choir and local activities. He ended by giving me every good wish.

The other letter was from Mum's favorite, Magada, I can still imagine Mum trying to say the name like a tongue-twister.

I have just got another set of films back from the developers and they're simply terrific. I have numbered my films since I left England and have taken 63 altogether, so now I will start to send them at intervals starting at film No. 1 which is me with one foot on the peak of the mountain on the edge of the desert.

There were a few disappointments at first, but the snaps it is taking now is making up for that. It is a terrific camera.

I have got some music out of the library and played it on a piano, there was a lot of Handel and Bach in it.

Last night I went down to the Fayid Education Centre to listen to a concert of recorded music for Good Friday. It lasted three hours with two intervals. I will send the programme with this letter.

The Concert Hall is a terrifically posh place, with a tiered stage for the orchestra, armchairs, carpets, a high roof and all sorts of carvings, decorated pillars, and a red curtain behind the stage behind which is the recording outfit.

I see Liverpool beat Sheffield yesterday. About time don't you think? I knew they wouldn't let us down, and I bet the result shook Keith, Ha, Ha!

This time last year they were all in KD, but it doesn't look as if we will go into KD for another week, although the fans have started.

I hope to hear some better news from all soon.

Much love to all,
David

March 1948
AG1(b) Branch
GHQ
M.E.L.F.

Dear Mum & Dad,

Today is very strange, the sun is not shining, yet it is only the afternoon. The reason is, CLOUDS, big white ones and the weather is considerably cooler.

We all hope that rain will come soon as water in this Company is only laid on between the hours of 6.30pm till 6.30am. But it doesn't really affect me, as the showers are on all day.

Nest Tuesday at the Fayid Education Centre is a concert of pianoforte music played by two English pianists. I may go.

How is St Hilary's going on? Has the warden left the church or just the choir and the organ? I am undecided whether to go back as a tenor, bass or what?

I have just received two letters brought down from work by the duty clerk for which many thanks. For something to write about I may as well comment on them.

First, Keith's letter. After translating, I see that he is fit enough to play "Rugby" which is just as bad as wrestling so he must by OK.

I also understood the detailed account of the School Certificate results which were rather surprising, I thought.

Now for Dad's letter. I rather like the project of going to fetch Moir (?) from Anglesey. Maybe we could both go, of course, all planning must be for during demob leave.

Are you writing to the cousin in America, three parcels is pretty good going, so I should think they would give you the energy to write?

I will start to make demob plans when the demob statement for 118 group comes out.

Demob statements come out about every three months and give the release dates of A/S groups up to a certain number. The last one came out three months ago and went up to group 100 (usually includes about 10 groups). The next one, due out next week, should go from 105-115.

The demob statement for my group should be out by Christmas, but the one next week should give me an idea to within a couple of weeks when I should be out.

Up to now I have been writing this letter for two days, adding bits on as I think. But I must finish now and get it ready for posting.

Much love to all
David xxx

PS Don't forget any negatives etc. Dad asks about health etc. Well, I am quite fit and as far as I know there is nothing at all wrong with me. It is now four months since I used a handkerchief, and six months since I washed one. David xxx

11th April 1948
AG1(b) Branch
GHQ
M.E.L.F.

Dear Mum & Dad,

Today is Sunday and I am lying back after a feast of cakes, buns and tea from the NAAFI 30 yards away.

Yesterday after work, we went to the Saturday matinee at the Cameronia and saw Laurel & Hardy and 'Escape to Happiness'. But as the picture we went really was not on (Temptation Harbour), so we had to go again in the evening.

Today it is as hot as ever. The sun is continually shining. Tomorrow, we go into K.D for good. Up to now is has been battledress at sundown, but now is the time when the weather never goes cold.

Have the sports stared at school yet? If they have, tell me who's going in for what? Also, who has left and who has gone in the army since I left?

How is the widening of Wallasey Village going on? I think I will give you a full-page lecture on the "wog"[10] (Egyptian native). We have decided that 'wog' means "Western Oriental Gentleman".

The Sweetwater Canal is known all over the world to carry every known disease. If a British or German soldier as much as puts his finger in it, he gets 37 injections straight away at the British Military Hospital, Kabrit.

The Sweetwater Canal runs through the wog village. When the 8am Port Tewfik – Suez – Ismailia – Port Said train passes there

---

10 This term, acknowledged as offensive today, was common parlance of the time in the context of this book. The author would no longer use the word but other instances have been left in this book for historical integrity.

are wogs in the roof, hanging on the buffers and crowded together on the sort of verandah at the rear, like in America.

Their idea of music is horrible. It is sort of a wailing chant and the expression on their faces is simply painful.

To finish off their language is the worst I have ever heard, there is no expression and no sound whatsoever.

Well, after that masterpiece, I think I will bash out a letter to Keith and Pat.

Much love,
David xxx

Bed,
Egypt,
11.30am

Dear Pat,

How are you – still alive after a scrap with Keith? I think it's about time you established your rights at the table.

Well, how's old Cabey/Caley [?], still ratty? And anyone else you may have decided to associate with. Who's your teacher at school and what's she like? Don't tell me, I can guess what you're going to say.

We have invented a new game called 'Monopoly' and it is played with money and property. You should have heard about it by now in the papers.

I see you're learning to pay hockey, handball & tennis. Well, I bet it will take you a long time to be good enough to beat me. The only trouble I find is that it is rather hard to grip all those wires on a tennis bat and hit the ball with the stick affair jutting out.

Love from David xx

14th April 1948
AG1(b) Branch
GHQ
M.E.L.F.

Dear Mum and Dad,

I waited to see if there was a letter this morning, but as there wasn't, I will attempt to think up something to say. Just about the weather, we go into KD on Monday as it is getting hot, the temperature is hovering about 85°F (cool).

I should think the "GEORGIC" is due to arrive Liverpool any moment now, so don't forget to let me know the approximate time of day of arrival.

Three of the members of our tent are at the pictures at the moment, the picture is "The Brothers", but as I have seen it in Wallasey I thought I might as well stay in tonight. There is the same routine here every day. Get up at 7am, start off to GHQ at 7.55am, get a paper, arrive at work at 8.15am (about the same distance as school). 10am to 10.30am NAAFI break. 1.15pm knock off work till following day. Play Monopoly or swim, or watch football for the rest of the day.

On Mondays, Wednesdays, and Fridays we go back to work by free bus at 5pm till 8pm, come back, get dinner and go to bed.

At choir we may attempt to do an Anthem, as I can help them with it, being sort of "experienced". What I am looking forward to now is to getting that parcel.

Well I think, seeing `as the candle is getting low, I may as well get into bed.

Much love to all,
David

15th April 1948
AG1(b) Branch
GHQ
M.E.L.F.

Dear Mum and Dad

At the moment I am sitting in the Lido Stadium waiting for a football match to start. It is the RE's Egypt v RASC Egypt. In nearly all these types of matches the game is almost as good as First Division. The teams usually have some professionals who have had to join the army.

At the moment the Basuto natives have just entered to entertain us with some music. They are in a special type of army-dress with bush hats. The weather is terrific, there are some white cotton-wool clouds about. The sun is warm, and there is a nice cool breeze. As for the scenery, at the far end of the field is a grove of palm trees. On the left is the Lido Club (a modern type of building).

The Basutos have now got into a march and have started with the drums like a tattoo. There is the drum-major, a massive native, swinging a stick and dressed with a red sash across his chest. The leading four drummers are dressed in leopard skins. They are a fine example of the British African Army. I forgot to mention they have all got red, white, blue, and yellow tassles and have white ropes tangling from the drums. They are all of the woolly-haired type, they have very dark skins, flat noses, and thick lips.

I forgot to bring the camera!

On the extreme right are the mountains and some green fields which are irrigated by water from the lake. Back in the camp I managed to get hold of a French book, which is a sort of grammar-conversation affair. I also got a geography book.

I haven't received a letter from you for eight days and I haven't received the parcel, but that will take a long time (about four weeks). It will arrive eventually.

I suppose you have heard about "DOV", which is Deferred Operationally Vital, relating to all Middle East RASC Clerks. At the moment release group 57 are 'DOV' as they should have been demobbed on March 14th. Deferrment in this way can be up to three months. But I don't, however, think that from group 100 onwards there will be any 'DOV'. The only reason for the deferment is the shortage of clerks. If you ask me, I think this is why we could not get in the Intelligence Corps. They are crying out for men for the Intelligence and Educaion Corps in the Middle East.

Could you send me some music that you can roll up by by air-mail, it isn't much. But I just sit by the piano and stare at an empty holder if front of me.

Well I think I will go to bed now, the result of the soccer match was 5-1 for the RASC.

Much love to all,
David

18th April 1948
AG1(b) Branch
GHQ
M.E.L.F.

Dear Mum and Dad,

Today is Sunday. This morning I went to choir, and we had our photos taken. Since then I have been lying down reading, drawing, or writing.

Last night I got hold of a spring bed which "Ginger" Caldwell had left while he is on leave, there are proper springs. This morning I woke up and had a cup of tea in bed (sheets, pillow etc), and then turned over and went to sleep as it was only 8am. I got up at 8.45 am, and went to breakfast, came back, got a wash, and shook my mat.

The flies are becoming a nuisance now, they keep landing on your arms, nose, ears, etc, all at the same time and it also, when you are trying to get washed, you will go to hit it, and cover yourself with water.

I don't think I have ever told you what we do and how GHQ works. I will give you an outline here. GHQ Middle East Land Forces controls all the countries in East Africa, Arabia, and the Mediterranean. To do this it is divided into three parts, "G" Branch," "AG" Branch, and "Q" Branch. "G" means General, and deals with operations and planning, secret weapons, chemical warfare, ordnance survey etc. "AG" means Adjutant General, and deals with pay, medical, welfare, organization etc.

"Q" means Quarter Master General, and deals with housing, feeding, and clothing of the soldiers. PYTHON is leave home for Regulars, and SEWLROM is Special End of War Leave Other Ranks. (f) deals with all family matters. That is a brief outline of GHQ.

How is choir getting on? Ask Keith for some more information and who is still in it. I will write again on Tuesday and post it Wednesday.

Much love to all,
David

21st April 1948
AG1(b) Branch
GHQ
M.E.L.F.

Dear Mum & Dad,

The first thing I will do will be to reply to your massive letter which I received three days ago. The main reason I haven't written for a while is the stamp situation. Price of airmail stamps rose today to 2½ d. I ran out of 1½ d stamps at the weekend and could not get any more.

I see the professor is out of bed now and that Pat is having her finger finished off, the news is a bit more cheerful than before.

On my previous letter, I sent a snap of myself & a snap in Ismailia. I am going to send all the snaps in numerical order, so let me know which number snaps you receive. For instance, the two I sent have nos 1&2 on the back. This is so I can keep a check.

I have not received any parcels yet, but they always come by seamail and take three weeks, could you let me know, when exactly did you send them.

It was rather a shock to read that Mrs Pearson has died. She was quite high spirited when I left. Have you seen Mr Pearson & Mavis?

Pat's writing is just the same as ever, and the grammar. Here's a bit of a gem for you: the people here consist of Egyptians, Sudanese (wooly hair types), English, French, Germans, Greeks, Spaniards, and negroes.

As for Keith's letter, screwy isn't the word. My knowledge of languages has risen considerably. I see you are getting good at French, eh! "Le vingt-deux mars" By gum!

Now you want those phlippin' questions answered. (You've had it):

1. Nickname of Chelsea is the 'Spurs' I think
2. Nickname of West Ham is *the Hammers* I think
   Arsenal – erm – hmm – ar! Yes! – no – no – NO!
   Everton – the blues
   Grimsby – The cup wallas
3. Edlington – Everton
   Matthews - Blackpool & ENGLAND
   Dick (Cocky) – Featherstone Rovers (Ha! Ha!)
   Woodruff – Wolves
   Topping – Tranmere or New Brighton
4. Gundar Haegg – 1 mile
   Hundmaar – 10 Mile
   Brown – 100 yards
   EH Liddell – 3 miles
   Hampson – 220 yards
   Macdonald Bailey – 100 yards
   Wycolf & Owens – 100 yards, 220 yards, 440 yards
   Archer – 100 yards hurdles
   SC Wooderson – 1 mile & 1000 metres (6 letters)
   Patton – Tennis
   Wint – 200 & 440 & 880 yards
   (To be continued)

I have just received another letter posted on the 22nd January. In it I see that you got a big food parcel from the USA.

You should be receiving another food parcel in about a months' time only I don't know what it will contain. Yesterday we were issued with KD and it fits me alright. It is the best KD that has been seen in the camp. We got three pairs long pants, two pairs shorts, three jackets, 1 belt, two strips of material for keeping the collar dry in the heat.

I will send a map of GHQ District to give you a better idea of the place.

Playing Monopoly, the day before yesterday, I won & ended up with £3,000.

Well, I suppose I'll have to pack up now and retire.

Much love to all,
David xxx

24th April 1948
AG1(b) Branch
GHQ
M.E.L.F.

Dear Mum & Dad,

I was hoping to receive a letter from you today but I didn't.

At the moment I am duty clerk at AG Branch and I have to receive 'phone calls, signals, messages, letters and open them. If they are addressed to the C in C, I have to open them, if they are addressed to General Sir John Crocker or marked 'Personal', 'Top Secret' or 'No 2 Inspectorate MPs & DBs', I leave them.

The weather is still terrific out here, not too hot, not too cold, the last roll of film I took came out perfect.

I think I will wait until I get a letter from you, then, probably, there will be something to write about. I am keeping fit and in good health, I haven't been ill at all since I left Wallasey on December 31st.

Much love to all
David xxx

25th April 1948
AG1(b) Branch
GHQ
M.E.L.F.

Dear Mum & Dad,

You will probably receive a letter to Magada along with this one. I thought it would be quicker to send it home first and then by airmail to Argentine. The best thing to do is to stick it in another envelope and put this address on:
 Magada Whort
 San Lorenzo 227
 Pergamino
 Provincia de Beunos Aires
 Republica ARGENTINA

I have almost got a complete set of civilian clothes except for a jacket so I will save up and get one. Don't send me mine as clothes are rationed in England and you are probably making good use of it at the moment.

Tonight (Sunday), we are probably going to play Monopoly. I hope to end up again owning the whole board and also half the bank.

Last night when I went for supper (not many go for supper) they just put the food out and you grab as much as you want. I got a few slices of some terrific pastry and meat, potatoes, gravy, cabbage, a plateful of pudding & custard and 20 bananas (of course I took some back to the tent).

While I was eating all this Handel's "Allegro Decizo" from the Water Music Suite came on the wireless.

I was listening to the cup final in the Coca Cola bar yesterday.

It sounded quite an exciting game, I had Manchester United to win (just a prophecy, not a bet), Anyway, they did 4-2.

Pete is getting everyone dumfounded with his 'mental telepathy' with cards. It is really humorous. He has big wide staring eyes, long fingers and is very thin. He gets you to pick a card and put it back. He shuffles the pack and deals till he comes to the card, all the time staring you in the face and at intervals waving his fingers like a hypnotist. He only looks about 15 years of age.

I am sending a couple of photos with this letter. They are:
- No.7: View from summit of Gebel Shawbrit southwards over POW camp & section of native village on the extreme middle right.
- No. 8: Me at the end of L'avenue du parc Ismailia. This boulevard is lined with palm trees and runs parallel with the Sweetwater Canal which is 50 yards to the left.
- No.9: A friend of mine in comparison with the rocks on the lower slopes of Gebel Shawbrit, Egypt.

Well, I think I will go for tea no so I will write again on Thursday.

Much love to all,
David xxx

Index to Photos:

First: I forgot to describe the six photos which I sent with the letter. There was one of the sports shop in the shopping centre, one of the Coca Cola bar (with parasols outside). One of the Cameronia cinema. One of me with the dog next door. One of two girls in shopping centre (taken at speed).

Those in this envelope are:
- Claremont Road, Wallasey
- Deepcut, Blackdown, Hants
- Claremont Road, Wallasey
- Pete with next door's dog
- Me
- Pete (afternoon siesta)
- Ian Simms, Bishopsgate, London, EC (looking towards Holborn and Cheapside) Taken when travelling from Blackdown to Thetford (January)
- Me on board the "SS OTRANTO"

14th May 1948
AG1(b) Branch
GHQ
M.E.L.F.

Dear Mum and Dad,

Many thanks for your letter which I received Saturday dated 9th May. Today is Whit Monday, and, as usual, it is a holiday in the Middle East.

Well over the weekend I have been to the pictures twice to see "The Spanish Main" and "Carnival" with Sally Gray. On Sunday I went swimming in the Great Bitter Lake and it was warm enough to be able to stay in as long as possible. As you will probably know, the sun is very hot now and we need as much salt as possible.

I received a letter from Aunty Ivy and Uncle Aubrey on Saturday, so I will reply as soon as possible.

We had an intake into GHQ on Thursday, and there are some blokes of A/S group 127. Amongst them is someone I knew at Chester Pte last September.

He also went to Blackdown with myself and Muggy Wray. He lives at Northwich and was held up getting back off re-embarkation leave, by the Winsford train crash. They all came out on the GEORGIC.

There is nothing else I can write about now. Believe me, it has almost wreaked my brain trying to think of what I have just written.

In your next letter send some questions so that I can answer them.

Much love to all,
David

May 1948
AG1(b) Branch
GHQ
M.E.L.F.

Dear Mum and Dad,

Very many thanks for parcel of papers, mags and comics, (the parcel was the one with the Liverpool Echo and the train crash), also a letter from Dad received yesterday and your letter received today.

At the moment I am up the NAAFI trying to keep cool under a fan. The weather is just such that it keeps you hot but not perspiring freely. If you relax you get a lot cooler. Temperature is about 90° F and rising steadily. KD goes in every two days to be washed and pressed.

Just received the evening paper so here is the latest temperatures:

- Alexandria – 72°
- Port Said – 82°
- Cairo – 86°
- Helwan – 97°
- Minia – 90°
- Asiut – 94°
- Luxor – 96°
- Aswan – 96°

The new hard-court tennis courts were opened today, but I have not been on today. Instead we played a short game of football, and it was rather warm.

In Alexandria, they are going to change the names of streets into Arabic as most are in French. I suppose all they will do will be to translate "Rue" into "Pasha".

By the way, the trousers I have got are fairly new second hand off Jimmy Fitzpatrick. If no-one is using my jacket and shoes you may as well send them on.

In the Winsford train crash I noticed there was someone called Mr H. Williams of Penrhyndeudraeth, do you think he is any relation to "Taffy", as he went there for an holiday once?

Well, I will write again on Sunday and post it Monday Morning.

Much love to all,
David

14th May 1948
AG1(b) Branch
GHQ
M.E.L.F.

Dear Mum and Dad,

At the moment I am in Dumbarton House reposing in one of the numerous, very comfortable armchairs which the various clubs in the district possess.

In this place is a big canteen, quiet room, library, writing room, gift shop, billiards and snooker, and table tennis.

Last night we went to the pictures and saw "Holiday Camp," a terrific British film.

We have received a letter from Ken Holmes who went on a demob a few weeks ago on board the "Cheshire." He arrived at Liverpool and was demobbed at York the same day. He arrived home at Loughborough, Leicestershire that night. Pete should be going any time now.

We have had a new intake, and in which the lowest demob group number is 118, and the highest 130.

I don't know if I even mentioned that Ken Holmes knew someone from 164? Wallasey Road, Wallasey, who went on demob as I came here. I don't know who he is.

I hope you are receiving my films alright. I have made out a list and given a number to every photograph I have taken in England and abroad. In my album are about 90 negatives, but, of course, not as many films.

I am reading a book called 'The Stolen Home Secretary,' and is also one of the best I have read so far. I am also reading a book called 'Spanish Commercial Correspondence.'

We have just thought about buying a "Crystal" radio set off the German POW's for about 15/-. I have heard they they are very successful (you know what the Germans are for making things.) Anything you want making, the Germans will do it very cheap.

In my last letter I sent a photo of Ray and Pete and an ATS. her name is Doris Allan, and she works in our office AG1(b). She comes from Perth (D'ye ken?). You can be sure she does nothing else but yap yap from one end of the day to the other. Still, '*Marleesh*,' as the Egyptians say.

I think I will now get some cakes and coffee. So I will write again on Wednesday.

Much love to all,
David

26th May 1948
AG1(b) Branch
GHQ
M.E.L.F.

Dear Mum and Dad,

Many thanks for your letters which I received Saturday morning. Everything is just the same here. Last night I put my civvies on and walked down to the Fayid Education to listen to a concert of vocal music which was preceded by Handel's 'The Faithful Shepherd'. (The piece of music originally advertised was 'The Entry of the Queen of Sheba').

After the concert I tried to see about advanced (University Standard) lessons in Spanish. But they just stared and said that the only person they know of in BTE[11], is a German P.O.W. who only teaches up to the Forces Preliminary exam standard, which is a lot lower than normal 'School Certificate'.

I read Dad's account of the ceremony in the new building with interest. I have only the vaguest memory of a few iron girders, so it seems that they must have 'stepped on the gas'. That will be the time when there are cakes on the table to eat at liberty.

I am glad you liked the parcel, although I hadn't the slightest idea what was going to be in it. It was just a "food parcel for the month of March" and there is one every three months, but we have to take it in turns as suppliers are limited.

I still haven't heard from the people in Cairo yet, I think it is getting a bit late. But in any case Cairo, Alexandria, Giza, Heliopolis, and the Delta are out of bounds until further notice owing to riots and the feast of Ramadan[12].

---

11 British Troops Egypt: includes all troops in Canal Zone and Egypt (80,000)
12 This is unclear; *Eid al-Fitr*; the Feast after Ramadan in 1948, started on 7th August

Of course none of that even happens here as the only Egyptians we have are labourers employed by us, and they are watched by armed guards everywhere they go. When British Troops occupied this region in January '47 it was entirely uninhabited.

I should think it rather unlikely that I might meet Ronald Duckworth. The aerodromes near us are "RAF Station FAYID," "FAYID NORTH," and "DEVERSOIR." We have RAF and Naval personnel employed in GHQ. In the B.M.E.O. (British Middle East Office), but I don't know where they are billeted.

The RAF stations I have mentioned are the only accessible ones from here. They are all on the road to Ismailia.

Pete has just come in and said that he feels certain that the RAF camp Berut (?) is at Kabrit not far down on the Suez Road. Kabrit is the home of the wireless and broadcasting station. Still, it is rather doubtful of ever meeting him.

Yesterday was the big thrill. A Vampire Jet aircraft did a demonstration flight over GHQ centred on the C-in-C's building 50 yards away from our office. It did all sorts of stunts from just skimming over our heads at 600 mph to looping at 5,000 feet up. The whine of the jets as it did a vertical climb was terrific.

"Time" here has its lapses. When I first came in the army we lived from day to day, then at Thetford it was from hour to hour. In GHQ at first it was from week to week. Now it is from month to month and I suppose after my leave it will be season to season.

We have managed to book accommodation at Port Fouad for 7-14th August, all there is left to do now is to get the pass signed. So I think, and I have also heard, that time flies after you leave.

Well, that seems to be the lot for now. I will write a bit quicker this week. For some queer reason last week I didn't know where I was, that is with this and that and the other.

Much love to all,
David

June 1948
AG1(b) Branch
GHQ
M.E.L.F.

Dear Mum and Dad,

Well, Dad, I think I can answer all your questions in your very welcome letter which I received yesterday.

We get meat in some form or another every day, sometimes it is quality more than quantity, and sometimes vice versa.

Bread is a bit dry and sometimes quite hard, but we can have as much as we want.

As for the amount, we are only satisfied, NOT full up. Meals usually contain a variety of concoctions which I have neither seen nor heard before, but they taste OK I have not the slightest idea how or with what the tea is made. (By the way, I am writing this letter on a book on my knee, the book is called "Dear Dead Lady").

I am not yet at the "sweating hard" stage and I have not yet taken much salt as a result.

As to holidays or free time, I have had four days for Easter, three days for Whit, one day Thursday 10th for the King's Birthday.

I am not yet due for leave, but in any case it will be too hot 'till September when I hope to take it.

The fact that we may be going to Kenya is very doubtful.

I have just received official information from the Egyptian Mail about the first of the fixed term army class release groups (I am Group 118).

- Group 101 will be demobbed 10-17 Nov. 48.
- Group 102 will be demobbed 18-26 Nov. 48.
- Group 103 will be demobbed 27 Nov. – 5 Dec. 48.
- Group 104 will be demobbed 6 Dec. 48?

Presuming this rate of release keeps steady, I should leave here about May 1949.

I got up this morning at the usual day off time of 8.30am, went for breakfast at 9am and got some ice cakes at 10am from the NAAFI. Since then I thought I'd read all day for a change. Soon the tangerine season will be here, and then big, juicy, sweet, tangerines are almost thrown at you. Up to now the seasons have been orange, coconut, ice-cold drinks, and soon the tangerine.

I have got another set of 16 prints taken at the Derby Day Fête, and as usual, everyone thinks they are terrific. Every time I show some films, I am asked, "what type is it?" "where d'you get it?" "how much?" "I bet it's English?" etc.

I will send the films as soon as possible.

Trying to see in this light is a bit difficult so I will write again on Saturday.

Much love to all,
David

June 1948
AG1(b) Branch
GHQ
M.E.L.F.

Dear Mum and Dad,

First, I believe it is Dad's birthday on Sunday 27th June, so "Many Happy Returns of the Day, Dad, and I hope the year will be a prosperous one."

I'm afraid the only birthday present I've got is the good news that I have passed an exam and have been upgraded to a 'Class 2' clerk. This now makes me eligible for promotion any time and a proper war office clerk.

For the exam I had to type 25 words a minute, for ten minutes, and also I had to know all about the interior workings of GHQ and war office.

I have just received a letter from Dad with a touch of Pat's handwork contained within, also I received a parcel of Wallasey News', a Knock-out, and a cartoon. Many thanks. There was quite a lot of interesting news in them.

I hope you are getting a phone in in August, or before I get home, if possible. Pete's just got a phone in at Worthing, and his number is Goring-on-Sea 46002?

It looks as if you are definitely going away this year at last, don't forget to send some postcards of Wales. I think the best day-trip would be a run from Garnedd Fawr to Llanberis in the Pass.

I remember that part of our cycle ride very well, we arrived at Llanberis at 7pm and arrived at the farm at 9.30pm. You'll find it just the same.

I'm afraid I couldn't write a very long letter last Sunday as I was in bed all day with tummy trouble.

I have still got some films to send and also the Derby Day programme.

By the way, July 1949 is the latest date by which we must be home, according to official reports. There is only a very slight chance that it will be changed, but we should be home before July.

They're closing down the office now, so...

Much love to all,
David

25th June 1948
AG1(b) Branch
GHQ
M.E.L.F.

Dear Mum and Dad,

A week on Saturday there are two good events on. The first is a concert of music by Handel, Bach, and Mozart, the time is at 8.15pm. The other is a Grand Cabaret and Dance at Fanara, a couple of miles down on the road to Suez.

In a minute I will be going to the NAAFI to get a big glass of tea and some egg rolls or sandwiches, you can always get as many eggs as you want. How are eggs in Wallasey?

I hope I will hear some more news about the week in Anglesey. You can guess that as I've been on a holiday every year, I'm going to miss it this year, but I will make up for it next year. Still it's about time you had one after six years.

I'll go up to the NAAFI now and continue after some eggs etc. After a nice feed of biscuits, (I didn't get eggs), I will continue.

I have just remembered my drawing, so I will send it home.

Yesterday, I went to the Bank and while I was there, a woman came in and cashed a cheque for £600. The cashier plonked wads of £5 notes on the counter and the woman stowed them in a black bag. My eyes bulged.

The Sunday paper Wallah has been round with all the English Sunday papers, I got the News of the World and the Sunday Graphic. The back page of the Sunday Graphic is covered in photographs of the latest Test Match, and in the News of the World is all the latest "Olympic" news. Well, I'll have to finish here.

Much love to all,
David

16th July 1948
AG1(b) Branch
GHQ
M.E.L.F.

Dear Mum and Dad,

It is with great pleasure that I received today, one parcel of civilian clothes containing jacket, shoes, and a shirt, I also received a parcel of newspapers and comics. And tonight I received two letters in one,

With it being payday into the bargain I had quite a hectic afternoon:

On finishing work at 1.15pm, I got a bus down to camp with the big parcel and papers, went for dinner at 1.50, got paid at 2.20pm. Then over to the office for the free cigarette issue which I sell for ten ackers (2/2d), (50 cigs out here cost 2/6d). After that at 2.50, back to the tent look at papers, make bed, go for a wash, come back, open civvy clothes parcel with everyone shouting 'spiv', and get a bus to work at 4 pm. I reckon now I've got about 296 days to go.

It is now Sunday and I have been down to the beach again for a swim. As usual the water was very warm. We went down for a swim yesterday as well, so I wore my civvies (coat as well).

I noticed that the contents of the pockets are just as I left them at Christmas.

The swimming trunks which I have had for three months were *buckshee* ("free" in Arabic) off Pete. He reckons he has now five weeks of D.O.V. to do (his group went long ago, but he was held back as 'operationally vital'.

A very funny thing happened tonight. Ray was lying on his bed reading when he heard some paper on his table rattle, he turned his head, and saw a few inches from his nose a mouse feeding on his packet of peanuts.

Last night, the film at the Cameronia was "So Well Remembered," not bad at all, a J. Arthur Rank production.

The weather here is still holding terrifically. It has been like a perfect English Summer's day for the past four months, and the sun hasn't gone in once. In England everyone would be going mad by now.

The mail is coming so erratically now that the weather in England must be very bad.

By the way Pat says she gave my address to Margaret Cochrane, well that's OK. I don't care who the b**** writes as long as I get a letter or something to read.

Well, that seems to be all for now, so…

Much love to all,
David

4th August 1948
AG1(b) Branch
GHQ
M.E.L.F.

Dear Mum and Dad,

Many thanks for a letter from Dad which I received yesterday. I sent a letter off to Keith this morning and also received one from him. He seems to be doing alright and getting up rather early (6.30am).

I was talking to a bloke who lives near Evesham but only goes there for weekends as he says the scenery there is the best in that part of England. He was quite interested in the W.G.S. camp.

So you think it's hot in England, well you ought to come to Fayid, the weather is quite bearable, 115° F.

I have just come back from Dumbarton House where I have been playing table tennis all night. Then we had two big cakes of chocolate and marzipan and afterwards, a hot cup of coffee.

On Saturday 7th August I will be going on leave. The food at Port Fouad is terrific and they have waiters. There are four of us going now, Ray, Ted and his friend, and me.

There is no moon tonight and it is therefore pitch black, except as usual, a cloudless sky and a lot of shooting stars.

I have still not heard from anyone in Cairo, so I have given up hope.

I will be taking my camera to Port Fouad, so you can be looking forward to a few films and I will get some taken in KD, for Dad.

There are five different ways of dressing in KD.

Well, I'm afraid there isn't much to say tonight, in fact, I just can't think, but I will write again on Sunday from Port Fouad, and will be able to tell you about the journey, the scenery, the place, and the food, as well as the joint towns of Port Said and Fouad.

Much love to all,
David

9th August 1948
AG1(b) Branch
GHQ
M.E.L.F.

Dear Mum and Dad,

Today is Wednesday and the leave up to now has been better than I dared to expect. The camp in Port Fouad is so good that you would hardly know any difference between it and a Butlin's Holiday Camp.

Anyhow, I suppose I had better start at the beginning:

On Saturday I finished work at 12.30 and went for Ray who works in S.T. Directorate. We walked down to the main gate of GHQ, and got out onto the Treaty Road. A lorry gave us a lift as far as Fayid Station and then we hailed a big truck as far as No. 9. B.A.D. (Base Ammunition Depot).

Then we got a lift in an ice-lorry to the Canal Road, another lift to the RAF Station, Deversoir, and then a 15 cwt took us into Moascar. We got a free bus to the station (Ismailia).

We waited 20 mins for the Port Said train and arrived at 6 pm.

There was a truck waiting for us at the station which took us straight on to the Ferry. We passed through the long tree-lined avenues of Port Fouad and arrived at Seaview Holiday Camp at 6.20.

We booked ourselves in and a wog offered to carry all my stuff to the tent, so that was a relief. In the tent are wardrobes and cupboards painted green, and also a washbowl in a stand.

Our tent is one of 20 in an enclosure on its own. As soon as we were settled in we went 100 yards to the dining hall, and when we walked in an Egyptian waiter pulled out our chairs for us at a table-for-four, he then dashed off and brought the first course which was Mutton Soup.

Glancing round, we saw that the room was decorated with paintings, pictures, flowers, curtains, blue-tiled floor, and the tables laid like you would find in Reeces Café, Liverpool.

There was butter, jam, and sugar in plenty, and if you want any more bread (fresh-bread), just call the waiter.

The second course was:
- A leg of chicken (a whole one)
- Boiled potatoes
- Stuffing
- Sausages
- Greens and
- Gravy

The third course was Jam rolls and custard. Then, of course, as many cups of tea as you want (the wog pours it out for you).

I think we must have been stunned by all this as we just sat and gazed for half-an-hour after it. The quality of the food was better than any café or restaurant I have ever been in on my cycle-rides or elsewhere.

In the evening we walked round the camp and came to a halt at the open-air dance-floor. On the stage, the "Culran Boys" were playing the latest Rhumbas in the Edmundo Ros style. They have been on every night up to now. The dance floor is lit up at night with red, blue, and green lights.

We went to bed at 10.30pm and woke up to find a hot cup of tea waiting for me, as well as clean shoes.

We visited the games hall after a slap-up breakfast. Here they have four large size Billiard and Snooker Tables in terrific condition.

We have played snooker every day up to now.

Then there are three table tennis tables, and every game under the sun, as well as jigsaws.

There is a library which is built in the most design (?), there is a music room where you can play any record you want, and also give in requests for the radio to play, (we have our own radio called "Radio Seaview.")

The piano room is next on the list, and is there for anyone.

We have our own beach on the Mediterranean Sea, and unlike the sea in most parts of the Nile Delta, it is clean and blue. There are two diving boards and two big rafts almost 100 yards out.

Adjoining our beach is the Residents' Beach which is for the use of the inhabitants of Port Said and Port Fouad. I was there yesterday and they had a Rhumba Band playing dance music.

The chief occupants of the dancefloor and the coloured sunshades were Spanish and French ladies, and also some Sudanese types.

Now for a description of our travels outside the Holiday Camp.

On Sunday night we decided to have a look around Port Said.

We left the camp and turned into one of the wide avenues typical of Port Fouad. This avenue is really much the same as Warren Drive but the trees are closer and have thicker foliage. Houses are massive and the latest modern, streamlined style set in massive gardens. They are the residence of all the rich Egyptians.

When we got to the ferry which is situated in a square something like Pier Head, Liverpool. The ferry (two funnels, single deck, transport carrying.) took us across the docks, a distance of about ¾ mile.

We passed through two barriers on the Port Said side and turned right into Rue Sultan Hassein.

We walked a few yards and arrived at the 'SIMON ARZT' store which is the biggest in Port Said. Inside it is exactly the same as Blackler's used to be, with a massive marble floor and glass cases all over.

On passing the toys section we saw a MECCANO set and Hornby trains (electric and clockwork) set out as in Lewises. There was also all the stuff you never see in England. There was tons and tons of chocolate in there, and no-one to buy it.

We walked on (after I bought a Conway Stewart, 14 Ct Gold Nib fountain pen) and turned left to the Britannia Club, which is the most luxurious club in the Middle East (according to my Guide). We had a snack, a look round, and then went up seven stories to the roof, from where we saw all over Port Said, including the docks and the entrance to the Suez Canal.

When we came out we made straight for the main street of the town, the Sharia Boulevard Farouk 1er. In this street, one mile long and very wide, we saw high buildings, French restaurants, Cabarets and Hotels. The predominant language is French, all the people you pass are French, mainly women.

The Boulevard Farouk 1er is like the Sharia Soliman Pacha in Cairo.

The other place we went to was De Lesseps Square, we only got there after I had asked three different persons in French how to get there. By time I get back I will be speaking it fluently, that is, like a native. At one of the cafés we had bread, butter, tea, three eggs, a lot of chips, for eight Ackers[13] ($1/8$).

There always seems to be much cooler breezes here than in Fayid, but the weather is still the same.

Well, I will finish off with a small map, and hoping that you are having a holiday at Garnedd either now or very soon. I repeat that my holiday is terrific up to now.

Much love to all,
David

---

13 Acker = originally used by British troops in Egypt as a name for the piastre: probably an alteration of Arabic fakka 'small change, coins'.

Well, I will finish off with a small map, & hoping that you are having a holiday at Gainedd either now or very soon. I repeat that my holiday is terrific up to now.

    Much love to all
    David xxxxxx
       xxxxx
       xxxxxx

P.S. Will write again on Sunday.

17th August 1948
AG1(b) Branch
GHQ
M.E.L.F.

Dear Mum & Dad,

We went to the pictures again last night and saw "A Likely Story", a surprisingly humorous American film. Wit it was Leon Errol in another funny film.

Where is Scott Street, Wallasey, because Butch who works in our office has relations there? He himself lives at Anfield, Liverpool 4.

Pete is going on Monday, but he said that as he would not be staying in Liverpool but going on to York, he would not be able to contact you. He will be sailing on the Empress of Australia, which berths in Liverpool.

At the moment he is got all his stuff out and is trying to work out how much stuff he can through the Customs.

I have just realized that I have to send this letter to Anglesey. By the time you get it you should be right in the middle of the holiday, either watching the care speed by or watch the cars watching you.

When you get on to the main road, imagine e & Monty cycling along if a year last summer.

Well, as I am not too sure if this letter will reach you, I will finish here.

Much love to all,
David xxx
PS I am using the pencil because I have just locked my pen away. D

17th August 1948
AG1(b) Branch
GHQ
M.E.L.F.

Dear Mum & Dad,

Just a few lines before I go to bed.

Yesterday I went as a Personal Assistant to the Major General NC Clowes DSO because his regular P.A. was ill. Now every time I go back to the tent everyone says: "How's the General?" But I am back in 1(b) again today as they have got a S/Sgt in as P.A. now.

I am sending another two photos, one of the ferry entrance at Port Fouad. (The ferry has two funnels like the Dover-Calais steamer). The other photo is of the Cathedral at Port Said). It is in one of the much quieter streets.

I was picked to play cricket for "A" services today, but I made a duck.

I (we) hope to be going somewhere at Christmas (Port Fouad or Port Said, or, if possible, Luxor.)

Well, Pete, Ray, Ginger seem to want the light out (9.30) so I had better finish.

Much love to all,
David xxx

22nd August 1948
AG1(b) Branch
GHQ
M.E.L.F.

Dear Mum & Dad,

Today is Saturday and I am up in GHQ as AG Branch Duty Clerk, but I finish at 9.15 tomorrow Sunday.

Pete is going in eight days' time (the Empress of Australia is the boat and it leaves Port Said on 30th August).

I am not sure yet if it is berthing at Liverpool, but I'll see if I can get him to ring up. He may have to go straight to the demob centre at York, which means that he will have no time in Liverpool.

Well, today is the start of the English football season, and up to now Everton have drawn with Newcastle United 3-3. (this game was played at Goodison on Saturday 21st August '48) I haven't had the results of Liverpool's match yet, I bet that Keith is shaken as I expect that he expected a 13-1 win (FYI Liverpool lost 2-1 away at Aston Villa).

But he may be sticking up for Liverpool this year to save being let down.

Well next Saturday Keith should get the School Cert results, so all we can do is wait.

Kabrit Radio is on the air (we do have a radio up here in this room) and there is a summary of the editorial from London. The subject at the moment is "Tobacco" and the fact that it is to be rationed. He says that the import of tobacco is more than before the war.

It is now Sunday and I have just come back from the pictures, where we saw "Song of Freedom" with Paul Robeson and

"Blockheads" with Laurel & Hardy.

After that we had four cream cakes and a coffee in Dumbarton House.

I have taken eight films (snaps) of the film in the camera, but I will have to the rest fairly soon as the film only lasts till November '48.

The last two photos I am sending are of the entrance to Suez by the causeway, and the other of the Mosque at Port Fouad. I have only seen the mosque from a distance, but to all the other places I have been.

We had the complete football results and I thought they were rather drastic.

I can't think of anything else to say now or any questions to ask, so I will finish till Tuesday and go to bed.

Much love to all
David xx

August 1948
AG1(b) Branch
GHQ
M.E.L.F.

Dear Mum and Dad,

Many thanks for letters and a parcel of S.C. papers from Keith plus a letter. I will send my version of some of the papers in my next letter and in due course return the papers.

I haven't heard from the people in Cairo yet, but when did they leave England, how long will they be there, and do you know their address? Cairo itself is now out of bounds to troops in uniform, and only passes will be given in special cases, for instance, passing through to Luxor or seeing relations or friends. Only a very small portion of Cairo is inbounds for special leave cases, that around "Sharia Soliman Pasha."

Last night at the Cameronia, we saw "Bad Men of the Border," and "House of Frankenstein," with Boris Karloff. I think the Frankenstein film was too interesting in a scientific way to be a horror film.

This morning I had to play the organ again in church. The place was crowded as the C-in-C, General Sir John Goeker, and the GO C-in-C Palestine, General MacMillan were there. Just think, two Generals depending on me. It's something to remember.

(*Continued after dinner*). I have just finished tea, for which we had, meat, beans, potatoes, gravy, and jam pastry roll for a sweet.

In the afternoon we all went down to the Lido for a swim, and the water was absolutely warm, so warm we had to go into fairly deep water where it was cooler. You get a bath in cooler water than that in England. But a swim serves its purpose, it does cool you down, wash the sweat off, and put salt in the skin.

During the afternoon a Sunderland flying boat just skimmed the roof of the Lido and carried on to Fanara Wharf, where we will be getting a visit by about four British visiting ships in turn.

The first ship in is HMS Liverpool. A representative football team will play GHQ sometime during the weeks' visit.

The children's festival has come round pretty quick. The last time I took two smashing photographs.

I'm glad to hear you are probably going into Snowdonia as far as Llanberis. A days trip there will be just right. Llanberis itself is at the foot of the Llanberis Pass and in wooded country, it is also the starting point of the Snowdonia Mountain Railway.

You will pass alongside a lake (Llyn Idwal) on the road before Llanberis, and from the foot of the lake you can see right up the Pass into the heart of Snowdonia.

Ted has just found out that we get 60 coupons on being demobbed, and no money for a suit. He has also found out that the 100 groups (release) will not be DOV which means we leave here about a week before the group starts demobbing in England. I reckon I've got about 300 days to do.

At the moment it is the Mohammedan Fasting Period [*Ramadan*][14], during which they are allowed to eat only between the hours of midnight and 5am, for 30 days. Then comes a feast [*Eid al-Fitr*][15]. If you go down to the village fairly late at night you will see dancing and singing going strong. As far as I can reckon, the native labourers in GHQ have about one hour's sleep per night.

Has Orange Peel taken over from Johnny Spencer for good, and where has the old boy gone?

Up in GHQ there is now an American Officer and an American Sergeant. The KD the sergeant wears (I have seen him quite a lot),

---

14 Start of Ramadan [1 Ramadan 1367 AH] was on Thursday 8 July 1948
15 Eid al-Fitr, also known as Meethi Eid, is the festival of breaking the fast of Ramadan

is rather spiv, and the hat the same. The stripes are upside down.

I don't know if you read in the papers about an accident that happened about 3rd July, when an Army lorry crashed into an armoured car. The driver of the lorry was killed, but the other bloke was only slightly injured and discharged from hospital. Well, the "other bloke" was Ted's brother (Corporal Hartfield of Wentworth Croydon). The first Ted knew about it was when I read it in the Egyptian Gazette last Sunday the fourth, at Timsa. When I told him, Ted said bitterly "Just like 'im, mad as an 'atter."

I have just realised that Dad's address is "Minus the air-raid shelter," well, I'm not sorry it has gone as it was obstructing the view.

The view here is sand, mountains, and sky.

Tonight, I hope to go to supper, write a letter to Magada, and read my "exciting" book, then after a *shwa shie* (*small tea* in arabic), recline beneath a sheet and try to conquer the heat for ten hours.

I hope the paper arrives safely as it will be very welcome.

I am sending a sketch of Llanberis and district, also a few photos which I have found in my wallet which were taken at the Derby Day Fête.

Well, that seems to be the lot, so I will write again on Tuesday or Wednesday.

Much love to all,
David

Overleaf is a map of Llanberis and surrounding areas

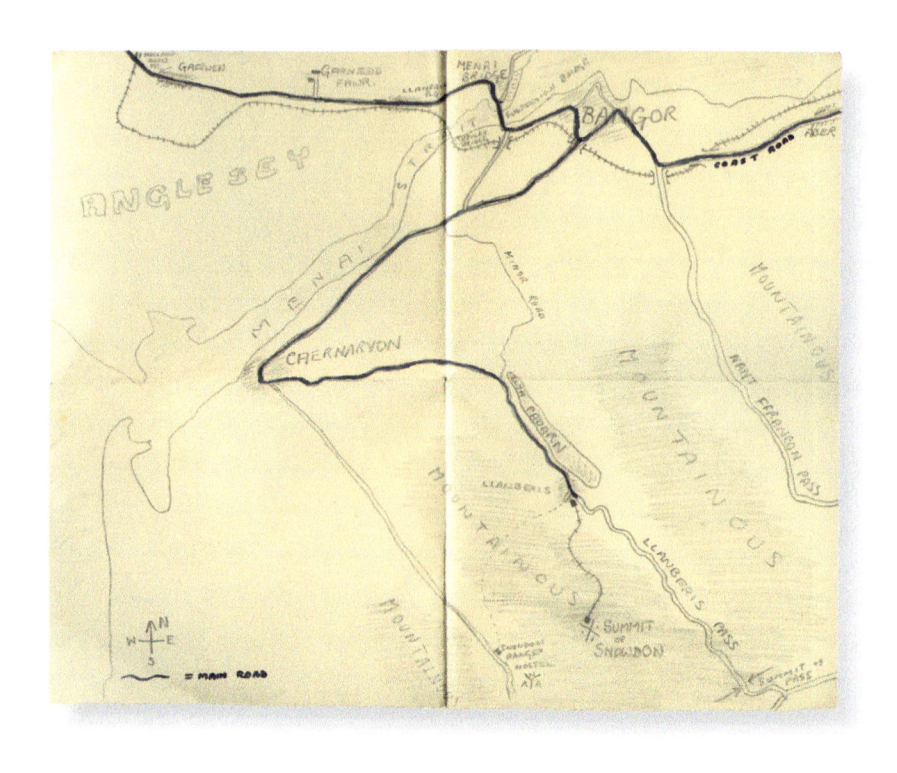

28th August 1948
AG1(b) Branch
GHQ
M.E.L.F.

Dear Mum & Dad,

The time is 7.35am and I am in a deserted office. The reason is that a bus leaves camp at 7am and 7.15am, but not later, and as I got up early and didn't feel like walking as it is rather a long way, I got the bus.

And when you come to think of it, it is better that sitting down in camp waiting for 7.45 when it is time to start walking. You see, I use my loaf.

Yesterday an officer asked me to print a big signboard, which I did. He was so pleased with it, he said: "Highly Commended" and went round showing it to all the other officers. Since then, I did another job for a different officer and he was so pleased that he went on talking for about a quarter of an hour on how good it was. (That was Major Read and he is being demobbed in England in October.)

Yesterday evening there was a choice of either going to the pictures to see "Black Memory" or of going to the Fayid Education Centre to listen to a programme of music by Bach (suite no:1 in D) (Piano Concerto in D minor) (Brandenburg Concerto No:3), all the best of his works. But the concert only started at 8.30 and would go on till 10.30, which is rather late, so I went to the pictures with the others.

Taffy has just arrived at the office. If you don't already know, He came here three months ago, and he comes from Abergavenny, S. Wales.

The weather here this morning is nice and cool and I have heard that it is abnormal for Egypt. Of course, the sun is always shining and we will be in the K.D. till November.

I am determined to go to the NAAFI early this morning so as to get some doughnuts and iced biscuits.

I see you are going away this weekend, so I suppose it will be alright to address a letter to Gardnedd Fawr, Angelsey.

What about the phone, is it anywhere near in yet? When do the kids go back to school? And the results of the School Cert?

Well, I hope this letter arrives before Saturday so that you will receive it.

Much love to all,
David xxx

23rd September 1948
AG1(b) Branch
GHQ
M.E.L.F.

Dear Mum and Dad,

Before I attempt to write a letter I would like to thank you all again very much for the parcel which arrived the day before yesterday. Contents were one bladder from Keith, autograph book from Pat, and the camera attachments which arrived safe and sound.

Yesterday I received a letter from Mum and today, a letter from Keith. I suppose if I were to reply in the same vein the letter would have to be strictly personal and top secret.

I got the films at last and am sending the four prints of me. The others aren't very interesting as they are mainly of other people. But I will send some more when I have more prints done.

Up at work, everything is going normal, but in a month's time I may have some very good news for you. But on the other hand I may not.

What I am going on is the fact that I am doing Chief Clerk of AG1(b) and have been for a week now. This morning, however, Mr Wade (Chief Clerk AG1), told me that Bill Dillon is not coming back to AG1, and that he would see if he could get me a bit of promotion.

Today I am on Duty Clerk at the Branch and I have to be up there at 8pm (it is now 7.15pm). All there is to do really is sit in the central point of AG Branch with the Duty Officer and deal with anything immediate that comes in. The advantages are: plenty of heat (two stoves and gallons of Keso), a wireless (and it is a good one), plenty of time to read or write letters in peace, and a decent wash basin in the morning. The only disadvantage is that you have to walk there twice, and back twice. Oh yes! And you also get meals in peace.

Paddy McGuigan has just come down with some mail and there is a certain letter for Taffy Davies which has a history. Almost three weeks ago Tony Collis got one of his local mags and showed us a group of three girls who were "May Queens" of Stoke-on-Trent. So for a bit of fun, Taffy, Harry and Dick got the address of the middle one which was under the photo and wrote. They signed it "From three lonely boys in the Middle East." A few days later they GOT A REPLY, and you ought to have seen their faces. Anyway Taffy wrote back straight away and now there is another letter waiting for him. Just goes to show, etc., as Mum would say.

He's reading it now and his face is all smiles.

Now back at the Branch, I am almost ready to go to bed, but first I must finish this letter.

Keith's letter was very interesting and informative in its own special way. I see that nearly the whole of Wallasey knows that I sent a Christmas Card to Phyllis. But you know the three quickest forms of dispatch: "Telegraph, Telephone, and Telewoman!"

I am now enclosing the four films, hoping that some more will follow soon. Also hoping that you may be send a few soon

Goodnight and much love to all,
David

24th September 1948
AG1(b) Branch
GHQ
M.E.L.F.

Dear Mum and Dad,

We have had word from Pete and he is home. That was his ship that Dad saw, it arrived on the Saturday night.

Well, as far as I know it took him ten hours to be demobbed at Aldershot from the time he got off the boat till the time he got on the train home.

I have now got a football, very strong and practically new.

I got the case off Ken Holmes when he went on demob, so yesterday I went up to the shopping centre and bought a bladder. I had the ball blown and laced properly there and then. If possible I will try and bring it home, but it should last till then.

There is no more definite news yet about demob but I think Christmas will be the turning point.

There is still no swimming in the Bitter Lake, but now that winter is approaching we do not miss it. The usual swimming periods are from April till September. Even through the winter it is as warm as any English summer. But to us it is cold in comparison.

I have just received a big fat letter for which many thanks indeed.

The negatives are "Just the job" and I intend to have them enlarged as soon as possible.

Everyone was interested in the small cut-out of the Echo about the 1000 troops for the Middle East. The situation here in GHQ is getting very critical owing to the lack of clerks. We did however get about 15 reinforcements into GHQ this evening. I think I know one of them who I saw from about 20 yards. He was at

Chester PTC[16] but was sent to the PDC (Physical Development Centre), on the other side of Chester. He lives somewhere near Tranmere.

Sgt Butcher lives at 46 ? Lipholme Road, Anfield, and I got hold of a book today which belonged to a T.M. Pemberton, Caldy Grange Grammar School, West Kirby, Wirral, Cheshire. I will…

letter ends there – missing page/s

---

16 PTC = Primary Training Corps

26th September 1948
AG1(b) Branch
GHQ
M.E.L.F.

Dear Mum & Dad,

As a continuation of my last letter I will now answer Dad's letter.

To me it seems that time has passed slowly since I was at B.T.D. Yet thinking of the time since I was at home, it has passed quickly.

The football results cam round this morning and I was surprised to see that Everton beat Preston North End by 4-1. Liverpool lost, New Brighton lost and Tranmere won.

Talking about sport I noticed an article in the Egyptian Gazette about a record being broken at the Guinea Gap Baths. I am enclosing the cutting (not enclosed).

I have just finished off the film with about 4 of me in K.D. so I will have them developed and the negatives sent home if they are good. If not, I have another film. I have decided to send home all negatives taken out here, so that you can keep them safely away.

There was a big dinner at Le Grand last night in honour of Major-General Murison who is relinquishing his appointment as M.G.A (Maj-General on charge of administration) and is handing over to Maj-General Cameron.

The picture tonight was "Les Miserables" with Charles Laughton and Frederick March. The story is by Victor Hugo. I was asked quite a few times 'what the picture was tonight' and when I pronounced it, they said "Eh?" so then I had to explain.

I have taken the film in to be developed and also a coule of negatives to be enlarged. The films will be ready on Tuesday night 28 of September, so you should receive the prints about Saturday the 2nd October or Monday the 4th October.

The pen I am writing with now is the one I lost 5 months ago, it is American made and still in good condition. I found it in one of the pockets of my battledress which I unearthed from sleep in the bottom of my kit-bag.

The next time I write, I will send some snaps and a few negatives.

By the way the conversation is trending in this tent at the moment I should think that the sooner the light goes out, the better.

So goodnight.

Much love to all,
David xxx

29th September 1948
AG1(b) Branch
GHQ
M.E.L.F.

Dear Mum & Dad,

Very many thanks for the parcel of newspapers etc. I was particularly interested in the booklet on Wallasey's Civic Week.

Bill and Butch were interested in the photographs of Liverpool & the ferries as they both come from Merseyside.

Whenever I get a parcel they sail over and "Any Echo's (sic), Dave?"

Of the 6 persons that work in AG1 (a) & (b) 3 come from Merseyside, one from Liverpool, one from Birkenhead and one from Wallasey. Taffy comes from Abergavenny, Monmouthshire.

The sweep last week was won by Cpl Burgess who had Notts County. I had Bournemouth.

The weather here is getting warmer for a while, but it is still very cool in the mornings. Temperatures are up to 100 degrees F again.

The Empress of Australia is leaving Port Said again with Group 74 DOV soon.

We have just been practising some carols (with Taffy only). Once we get together we put on some terrific singing. We have quite an audience at times.

If we get another desk in here I will try and get another week's leave in January or February.

I have just heard a bird whistling. We never have any kind of bird life here being in the Middle of the desert, so it does sound rather queer. What we do here is only the sparrow.

I had intended to put the photos inside this letter but I forgot them and left them down in camp. I will send them on tomorrow, but first, I will warn you that they are not much good. So I will get some more to be taken as soon as possible.

Time is drawing near so I must finish this letter.

Much love to all
David xxx

4th October 1948
AG1(b) Branch
GHQ
M.E.L.F.

Dear Mum & Dad,

Many thanks to Keith for letter received this morning. It gave me a lot of the news I have been wanting for a long time. Who is Ivy B?

I have someone who I think lives in Sandy Lane, he used to go to Aldershaw and I think he is the brother of Enid Walker. He is a small bloke, darkish hair, tendency to walk mickey-toed. I never have time to find out so I hope you can find out at home if it is him. As far as I know he works in G.H.Q.

The other person who lived in Leasowe Road, but who I never had a chance to speak to has gone on demob.

The weather is now cold in the mornings and evening. IT is thus only slightly hotter than a warm summer day in England. When the temperature gets to about normal English summer type, we change into battledress, that will be about the middle of November.

The picture last night was "The Prisoner of Shark Island" which I saw previously at the "Odeon", Woking, near London.

I have just seen the largest mobile canteen in the Middle East, a complete sports shop, outfitters, general and buffet. It was parked by the Naafi and is 56 feet long, and as wide as a British Railway carriage.

G.H.Q is running so short of clerks that they are bringing in civilians to take their places as they go on demob.

As far as I know the demob benefits I get are 1 day's leave for every month in the Army. No civilian clothes, but 60 coupons and no money to buy clothes.

I am hoping to get a job before the 22 days are up.

Well, we go to work again at 4 o'clock to start at 5. We finish as 8pm and get some dinner. By then it is too late to do anything.

Much love to all,
David xxx

7th October 1948
AG1(b) Branch
GHQ
M.E.L.F.

Dear Mum & Dad,

Many thanks for Dad's letter received yesterday. It was very good news about Dad's rise, all he wants now is a title.

It is doubtful about the news rates of release of A/S Groups as the release programme has not come out yet. But as soon as it does, I will be one of the first to see it, being on Release, Python, Liap, Sewbrom, Lilop. I think nearly every clerk in G.H.Q would love the job I've got. It is assumed that 101 will be demobbed between the 7 and 14 February.

There are now 95 pin ups in this tent, adorning the roof mainly. Some of them are really horrible.

We have just been having a discussion and an intelligence quiz. Two of us, me and another bloke< the most intelligent in the tent, had them all well out of their depth.

We managed to stress the fact that the more a person swears (9 out of 10 do here), the less intelligent he shows himself, because he does not know any phrase or word to replace it. He thus has a very small vocabulary and is not able to express himself.

But in the British Army this does not make the slightest difference. For some reason, a person with brawn is liked better than a person with brains.

The enclosed cutting (Nothing enclosed) is from the Egyptian Mail dated about the 1st October 48. I suppose you will know about theses proposals.

Capt Leete left by plane for Cape Town yesterday morning at 0600 hours. He was married a couple of months ago and is being demobbed in Cape Town with his wife.

For supper tonight they brought out a bathful of bananas and I managed to eat 12 of them. Also for supper we had meat, tomatoes and beetroot, with some cake.

Not much to report about the weather, it is still the same as usual, that is much cooler than at the middle of summer. Last year battledress was only worn morning, noon and night, from the 7 of December till the middle of April (1948).

I still Haven't used a handkerchief for months, if I even forget to take one to work it never worries me in the least.

Well, I think I'll go to bed now as it is almost 2030 hours (8.30pm Egyptian time – 6.30 Greenwich Mean Time). I will write again at the weekend.

Much love to all,
David xxx

10th October 1948
AG1(b) Branch
GHQ
M.E.L.F.

Dear Mum & Dad,

With lses than 11 weeks to go till Christmas, and the news gets worse every day. Now the demi-official news is that all conscripts will serve 2 years, which means that next September is the earliest you can hope for me to be home. I think you had better let me have the English end of the news, and also about the political situation.

To counteract this news, I think I should have some good news for you in a few weeks' time, but don't depend on the fact that it will come.

Tony Collis has just got spivved up in a complete civvy rigout so as to go the skating rink. Dick Bradley, Harry Fryer and Jack Hewitt have gone to the Cameronia, I have stayed in tonight and Taffy Davies has got a sty (sic) in his eye, and he looks as if he has been in a real scrap.

I thought Keith was in the men's choir now, but in his diagram, he was in the boys'. Is he in a club or does he contemplate the idea of being a leader?

It is now 5 whole months since we had any rain, and 5 months since I used a handerkerchief. Also, I have just had my first orange for 5 months, so they must be coming into season again.

The sweep this week was won by a bloke called Chapman from AG15 who had "Motherwell", which got 8 goals. Liverpool drew with Chelsea, Tranmere drew with Chester. Everton lost, and New Brighton lost.

It is…

Saved, have just received your letter with Pat and her "5" which is quite good, and by the sounds of the letter I should be getting many more in the near future.

I was almost wallowing in shallow water then as every topic was exhausted.

I see that Keith is now playing for the first XI, but the amount he alters in such a small time, I don't know whether to pity him, or the opposing team.

I forgot all about the fact that the shelter had been taken away and with it, I suppose, re concrete floor. But, every little helps. And with Dad on the go… well… Goodnight.

Much love to all,
David xxx

October 1948
AG1(b) Branch
GHQ
M.E.L.F.

Dear Mum and Dad,

On Saturday I bought a watch for £3-15-0. It is Swiss made and has 15 jewels, the colour is a blueish grey and the watch is squat (?) and streamlined.

At work the two people that run "Registry" are ill in bed, and so I had to do the management for a day. I think I am regarded as the only person that can do anything in AG Branch.

AG1(b) had to have me back as they had too much work to cope with, and AG1(a) have now got an extra clerk.

Next Saturday there is a cabaret and dance at Fanara, so I think we are all going to it. But also on Saturday night is a programme of recorded music by Handel, Bach, and Mozart.

We have also another adventure for the weekend, Lake Timsa Holiday Camp. The Holiday Camp's attraction is the food, it is terrific, so either my stomach will take me to Lake Timsa, or my head to Fanara. Somehow, I think my stomach will take preference, especially as they have butter and jam on the table.

This morning 73 group went on demob. When I first arrived 66 group was going out.

At the moment we are teaching each other Arabic. Here are a few words:

Alakeefik = I don't care
Bardin = later
Buccra = tomorrow
Buckshee = free
Shware = a little

Mefish Falouse = No money
Kam Falouse = How much?

About films, I have sent practically all the interesting ones home, I have hardly any left. Also, subjects are well-nigh exhausted, and as cameras are now forbidden anywhere outside GHQ there is not much left to take.

The weather has gone a lot cooler lately, Pete says it is unusual as it gets hotter and hotter up till August. But we are now at the beginning of the KHAMSIN period, a period of small whirlwinds of which we have already experienced one. It was a high funnel of sand with a high wind velocity. This region averages one strong whirlwind in a year. With this short cool spell the flies seem to have diminished, thank goodness.

My earthenware pot is empty, so I will fill it before going to bed. It keeps water ice-cold in this climate. It is a funny thing, but where in England cold water is bad for you when you are hot, yet out here we are told to drink as much cold water as we feel like, as it is good for health.

Well, my watch says 9.42pm so I will fill my water bottle and go to bed.

Goodnight and much love to all,
David

14th October 1948
AG1(b) Branch
GHQ
M.E.L.F.

Dear Mum and Dad,

And about time, don't you think. This morning, I was told that the Board set yesterday and I am now a Paid Acting L/Cpl with effect from 1st September 1948. So that all back pay is in credits.

Yesterday, outside the cookhouse, I met Roy Walker, Enid Walker's brother from Sandy Lane. He seemed rather surprised to see me and he couldn't quite think who I was, but when I said "Do you know Keith Howard?" then he knew. You remember every morning I used to pass him on the way to school, usually at about 9-10am.

Anyhow, he sleeps in 4 Coy[17], about 100 yards away. It is the same Coy that Barry Walker (no relation whatever) from Leasowe Road was in. Coincidence isn't it?

The weather has gone very cold for the last couple of days, and it looks as if it may continue. When I came out of the pictures on Tuesday night (the picture was "Vice Versa"), my thumb was numb.

Bill Dillon says that if the weather keeps up like this we will be in BD[18] by the beginning of November. I am taking my BD jacket to the tailor to have the tapes put on.

Yesterday morning I had my first mile run since I came out here, but I did it alright, and as usual, I was overtaking wholesale, while people were red in the face, and puffing and panting, my

---
17 Coy = Company (military unit)
18 BD = Battle Dress

legs were a bit stiff after it, but otherwise it was OK.

With some more practice I should get back into form again.

I have just taken the two Wallasey News' over to Roy, but as he wasn't in, I left them there. He is 127 group.

Up at work, any present job is dealing with Release, Python, Lilop, Sewbrom, and D.O.V plus all kinds of Release defessments, voluntary or otherwise.

There is a lot more to it than before. I have to see that Commands submit their returns and applications etc: DOV returns to be submitted twice a month, and officers Python Returns from the Middle East and Nairobi (East Africa Comd). I also have the power to draft letters and signals to War Office. The responsibility of the job is a Sergeant's.

But the establishment of GHQ is being cut down and it may come down to a full corporal, but even that is not too bad. I am hoping for something but I won't tell you as it is quite possible that it won't come off. Well, anyhow, I may as well.

I hope to be transferred along with my job to AG1(c) where I would most probably take over Chief Clerk (S/Sgt). But, of course, it is not likely, only a rumour.

Latest news about demob is that 74 group DOV, went on demob this morning.

50 of them in two buses passed us on the way to work and they yelled like hooligans at us, we watched until they were out of sight on the Treaty Road to Fayid Station.

The boat is the "ORDUNA", bound for Liverpool. I know quite a few on it, including a bloke from St Helens. *(Interval for a bar of Cadbury's blended chocolate)*

I have just been reading the Overseas Daily Mirror, and in it was a picture of a soldier at Catterick Camp taking a pot shie at a local fair. Under the picture was "Signalman Derek Wardle, 19." *(Interval for tea)*

Tea consisted of meat, gravy, potatoes, peas, and rice pudding which was quite nice.

A few days ago I got some cycling magazines from Tony Collis. They are dated about May and June '48, and of course, bring back memories.

He himself was more of the sports type of cyclist as opposed to the tourist like me and Monty. *(Interval for supper)*

Tomorrow is Friday and Payday.

As that is all the news for now I may as well get into bed before I freeze, so…

Much love to all,
David

19th October 1948
AG1(b) Branch
GHQ
M.E.L.F.

Dear Mum & Dad,

I had a bit of a windfall last night, in the form of 2/6d worth of stamps. You see when I came out here, I met a bloke called Ken Acors, and on the ship, I took some photos for him. He gave me his home address in England, which is in Romford, Essex. Last week I sent the films and last night his mother wrote back thanking me for them and enclosed the stamps saying that they would probably come in useful. Ken Acors is now stationed at Petrol Depot at Benghazi in Cyrenaica[19].

What is the weather like in England? How would you like to wear as little as possible at this season like us, as the weather has been warmer this weekend?

The train bound for Port Said has just passed. They sound like the 'Flying Scotsman' but I think top-speed is in the region of 30mph.

There are four main railway lines in Egypt. Namely: Luxor – Cairo – Alexandria. Port Said – Cairo and Port Said – Suez.

Football matches have started at the Lido again. Next Saturday there is a routine match, and Sunday is a match between R.A.S.C Egypt, and ?

The last of the speedway trials was run today at the Olympia Stadium, Fayid. The entrance programmes were numbered and in the draw the winner got a motor-bike or £190. A guardsman won it and dashed across the stadium in full view of everyone to get it.

---

19 Cyrenaica was an administrative division of Italian Libya from 1927 until 1943

"Butch" won the sweep this week with Notts County. I had Manchester City.

I see New Brighton lost, and Everton did not do to badly against the league runners up, Derby County. Liverpool won and so did Tranmere.

We have heard nothing more about demob yet, but 75 Group DOV are going in a couple of weeks' time. By next Easter, Release in the 100 groups will be in full swing.

With 108 Group out, it will seem a lot nearer. Almost all my friends are between 110 and 114, and every time one goes, I know that it is nearer.

Tony, Jack and myself have stayed in tonight while the other three have gone to see "Roar of the Press" and "I Killed That Man".

We are only 100 yards from the skating-rink and the music is always the same every night. Sound travels a long way in this country.

I hope to get a letter tomorrow but I can't think of anything to say, we usually pool substance in the tent. Each of us thinks of something to write about and we do get on quite well sometimes.

Much love to all
David xxx

P.S. On reading this letter over I find it is very disjointed but… perhaps it is lack of detail which is very scarce. D.

20th October 1948
AG1(b) Branch
GHQ
M.E.L.F.

Dear Mum and Dad,

Many thanks for both letters received this morning. Taking Mum's letters first, I will attempt to comment as there is no fresh news from here.

My shoes are getting on fine, although I have just started on the shoes you sent out with my sports jacket. I can get the other pair soled and heeled in three days for 30 Ackers (6/6d).

At night here it gets dark in about a quarter of an hour, which is now between 5.45pm and 6pm. The only lights on the way back from work are those headlamps of cars, the lights of the C-in-C's gate (second entrance to G.H.Q.), and the shopping centre which is very well lit up. The ground is very uneven, but by now we know almost every bump in the ground.

It seems rather abnormal to be able to get "Curtains dry in a day." Here I can wash and press a shirt in 20 minutes, and have a pair of clean socks in ten minutes. Handkerchiefs are dry before we get back to the tent (20 yards).

Dinner time we have two more bathfuls of bananas, and as usual we helped ourselves to a couple of platefuls.

I'm afraid we don't catch kippers in the Bitter Lake, Dad, but once or twice we are able to get one out of the NAAFI.

The tent was interested in your views on the political situation, of course, I paraphrased it. Latest unconfirmed reports state that we are to do dead on two years in the Army. The next release programme should give us a rough idea, as groups 76-110 should be given. April should see the release dates of 118 group.
I believe Roy Walker is 127 group.

I've just got hold of a couple of books on the Olympic Games: One is "Olympiad 1948" with a summary of Games and all Olympic records since 1896. The other is "The London Olympic Games", which is a programme and a visitors guide and also contains the records. Cost 2/6d each in England (I got them free, of course).

Also the Cricket Annual for 1948 is now my property.

Pat Leash (two tents away) is playing his clarinet. He is the leader of the GHQ Dance Band and can he play.

Christmas is nine weeks on Saturday. Ron (s/sgt Scott) thinks he is going on demob on the "Empire Trooper" to Southampton on 1st Nov.

If you saw the position I'm in finishing this letter you'd begin to wonder. I started sitting up with pad on my knee.

Much love to all,
David

24th October 1948
AG1(b) Branch
GHQ
M.E.L.F.

Dear Mum and Dad,

Many thanks for Dad's letter received this morning.

I told Jack of the possible pen-friend, Edith Jones, and he seemed happy enough. I don't know how many times he has asked me "when do you think you'll get a letter?"

The football match at the Lido this afternoon was hopeless (?), the teams were the Possibles v Probables, but the nickname after the match was, the Impossibles v Improbables.

The rumours floating round this camp are optimistic. Jack, 105 group, hopes to be out by the beginning of March, and I have heard that I should be out any time between July and September, as they will have to pass a new bill to keep us in over two years.

continued 25th October 1948

Jack has just had a letter from Edith Jones, and he seems pleased with it. He is writing back tonight, and wants a photo, so you can warn her if you like. By the time you get this letter she will probably get Jack's.

It is rumoured that we go into battle-dress on Monday, in the evenings only. But we all think that it is still too hot to wear anythink (sic) except K.D. shirt and slacks. The weather has gone considerably warmer again and some people have had slight touches of prickly heat.

There have been a few changes at the office. An ATS Corporal has just taken over AG1(c), and another ATS private has come into the office to do all the typing.

In AG1(f) they have got an Italian civilian girl typist, and I believe she speaks Spanish, but as usual, it is just an unconfirmed report.

Shortage of clerks in GHQ is so acute that there are now more civilians than British soldiers. This, at least, helps to brighten things up a bit.

All the girls wear the latest fashion and hair styles. In this part of the world, we are about as near to civvy street as we could possibly get.

In three of the magazines you sent there are some very good technicolour scenery pictures, and I have been asked to get them up.

Latest news about release is that 75 group DOV may be leaving this Sunday 31st October.

Among those who will be going are all the Chief Clerks of AG 1 sub sections. There is our Chief Clerk s/sgt Scott, RASC. AG1(b), s/sgt Butcher RASC, (homeward bound for Liverpool) AG1 (A and MP), Cpl Parfrey, the dozey Chief Clerk of AG1(c), and also s/sgt Crosscand, Chief Clerk AG1(f).

There is a very strange thing about the above-mentioned persons. THEY ALL HAVE GINGER HAIR.

The ship will be the Empire Trooper bound for Southampton for a change.

The films this weekend were "Shop at Sly Corner" and "Personal Column," with Sir Cedric Hardwick, who, I noticed, is (or was) on at the Royal Court Theatre, Liverpool.

I'm sure there was something else, but as I can't think, I'll remember it for my next letter. Goodnight…

Much love to all,
David

29th October 1948
AG1(b) Branch
GHQ
M.E.L.F.

Dear Mum & Dad,

Today is Friday and we have just been paid. I haven't been able to write for four days as there has been absolutely nothing to write about.

75 Group which was to have gone on demob on Monday will not be going now until a week on Monday, so I think we will go to Liverpool.

Ron, therefore, will be staying as Chief Clerk for another week.

I read something in the Egyptian Mail about 45 WRENS who embarked at Liverpool for GHQ. They will go to the office of the principal Naval Staff Officer mainly. The office is by the BMEO (British Middle East Office).

There was a big crash on the Treaty Road by the GHQ main gates about two days ago. A 15-cwt truck had a head-on collision with a three tonner. An officer was killed and the driver is not expected to live.

I am continuing in pencil as I have just locked my fountain pens away.

It is now known definitely that Ron & 75 Group DOV (?) are sailing on Monday 8th on board the Empress of Australia. It is calling at Famagusta (Cyprus), Salonika, Piraeus, Malta, Gibraltar and Liverpool.

I will send a rough map of GHQ, but it has by no means got all the branches, of which there are 75.

S.M.C is the STAFF MESSAGE CONTROL from where all signals are sent to be dispatched (Radio station is between GHQ and the aerodrome one mile away.)

I don't know what to do this weekend, there is always the pictures, and the football, the speedway etc.

When does Dad start work in the new building at the top of James Street? Last time he said the machines had still to be put in. Erm… Hmm…

Well, on Monday night we go into Battledress and on the 22nd it will be worn all day long.

I must go to be now, so I will write again over the weekend. Good night

Much love to all,
David xxx

29th October 1948
AG1(b) Branch
GHQ
M.E.L.F.

I am writing this letter in the MMG Club, Fayid, after a terrific supper. The club is 150 yards on the main road from the Cameronia towards Suez. The lounge here is just like an enlarged sitting room, and there is usually a log fire. Of course, there is a wireless as well.

How is the choir going and who does the solos now etc? Does the new bloke know how to play the organ? Is he as good as Mr J.D. Howard?

In a couple of weeks' time, I will be the second person from AGI to go on demob, Pat Leask being the first 110 Group.

The strength of AGI is 14 OR's

AGI (a)	Taffy Smith (Sgt) regular
	Pat Leask (L/Cpl) 110
	Taffy ? (Pte) 138
AGI (MP)	Johnny Burton (Pte) 128
	Jack Boyles (Pte) Regular
AGI (b)	Dave Howard (L/Cpl) 118
	Alan Stevenson (Pte) 139
	Johnny O'Neill (Pte) 137
AGI (c)	Mary Lodge (Sgt) ATS Regular
	Mary Stewart (Pte) ATS Regular
AGI (f)	? (Pte) Regular
	? (Pte) Regular

Margaret Stevenson (Pte) ATS Regular

Two civilian typists on one-year contracts finish November 1949.

       Mr George Hawa AGI (b) & (c)
       Miss ? ? AGI (f) (Italian)

And finally, is George Wade (WO I) regular, Chief Clerk of AGI.

   Tomorrow is the big job of moving, we have to vacate some huts for the Joint Planning Office and fill some of the half empty ones.

Much love to all,
David xxx

2nd November 1948
AG1(b) Branch
GHQ
M.E.L.F.

Dear Mum & Dad,

Tonight's mail is just coming in, on two wings and four propellers. The plane just passed over the tent with about 100 feet to spare. The undercarriage is down and it is circling to land at one of the longest Middle East 'dromes, one mile away. (RAF FAYID)

Jack has had three letters this morning, one from Maureen, one from another girl in Hoylake, and one from Edith. They all came by sea, except the one from Edith. I thought I would let you know about this as a 2½ d stamp takes two to three weeks to arrive.

Last night we went into Battledress and the heat was stifling. Everyone was complaining of prickly skin and the heat. When we got to work, we could hardly move, but it wasn't so bad at 8pm. We go permanently into BD on 22nd Nov. Even now at 5.15pm, all I'm wearing is a pair of P.T shorts and I'm still almost sweating sitting down. The flies, as usual, are terrible.

There is nothing much happening at work. Ron goes on the Empress of Australia next Monday or Tuesday bound for Liverpool. Release news is still at a standstill, but I believe that the new Release programme has been received in G.H.Q. probably only by Grade I staff officers (General Sir John Crocker, the 11 Major-Generals and the *buck-shee* Brigadiers. Buck-shee is an Arabic word and if I can remember rightly, I used to know it in England before I came out here.

I have just met another bloke out here who was at the Dale, Chester, with me. His name is Miller and he works as a Surveyor at the Survey Directorate, GHQ. He also is in 4 Coy and also in the Royal Engineers. His rank is Sapper (Pte).

I have just been giving Jack a lecture on Merseyside, what it is composed of, and what it does. No-one I knew here, has ever heard of Wallasey until I came.

It is now almost seven weeks to Christmas and from what I have heard it is not much different to any other day out here, so I think I will go into Ismailia and see the French. The Wogs had their Christmas round about August. Next Christmas, if everything goes well, I will be having a good time in Wallasey and preparing for my 21st.

I know what Mum would say. "Ooh! Doesn't time fly" "Mum" "Yes it does, doesn't it?" "I was only saying yesterday it doesn't seem a week ago since he left school" "Ah well, they're all the same aren't they." "Mum" "Yes" "Oh Yes" (Conversation with Mrs Hughes). "As true as I've got these keys in me 'and."

The mail plane must have been successful, as the duty NCO has just come with the news that the mail has arrived at the Branch. Of course, I won't see till tomorrow if there is any for me.

But this letter will have to be sealed tonight as the mail leaves the Branch for the APO every day at 8.30am.

So Goodnight…

Much love to all
David xxx

4th November 1948
AG1(b) Branch
GHQ
M.E.L.F.

Dear Mum and Dad,

Many thanks for a combined letter from Dad and Pat and also a parcel of newspapers including a Lilliput[20]. From what Pat says it seems that you have received a second food parcel. Is that right?

I got the photos alright and there is one that has never been developed. It is the one taken about half way down the West Side of Loch Lomond in Perthshire, Scotland.

The temperature is again in the region of 100°F, and we are all wearing as little as possible. It seems that because we have gone partly into Battledress the weather has chosen to warm up a bit.

I suppose the preparations for Christmas are in full swing in Wallasey, cotton wool and silver paper in the windows etc etc. out here it might just as well be May for there are non whatsoever. As I said before I am definitely not staying in Camp over Christmas. Ismalia's the place.

I think the LOA (Local Overseas Allowance) is going up from 6d to 9d per day in about three weeks time, and together with my L/Cpl's pay which is almost through, (all money from 1st Sep in credits), I am doing alright. I always keep quiet about how much money I have, if the others are broke, so am I, and they always are by Tuesday. I don't know what people spend their money on.

What are Keith's views on smoking and drinking? Now that he is going to the club, there will be a strong temptation to smoke,

---

20 Lilliput = a small-format British monthly magazine of humour, short stories, photographs and the arts

like I had. When Dad said the argument was damn awful, I didn't know whether you meant the noise or Keith's attitude.

Knowing Keith and his size I should think it was the noise. How's his feet?

Ron has just been in the tent and says that next Tuesday he is getting up at 4.30am and will catch the 8.15am train to Port Said.

Jack has just gone across to supper, and he will be bringing me a cup of cocoa before I go to bed in about 90 mins time. Today, Thursday was one of our half-days and there was not much work in this morning.

The following is how work gets to me. GHQ deals mainly with War Office, and next HQ East Africa Cmd, HQ Malta Garrison, HQ Tripolitania, HQ Cyrenaica, HQ Cyprus, HQ British Forces ADEN, BMM to Greece, BMM to Saudi Arabia, BMM to Ethiopia, HQ troops Sudan, and at one time HQ Palestine. HQ BTE (British Troops Egypt) also comes under our command.

Mail from these sub-HG's comes into GHQ and to Central Registry where it is stamped, booked in, and put in Branch pidgeon holes for distribution according to subject. All mail for AG Branch comes into AG Registry where it is again sorted further for Sections (AG1, AG2, AG3, AG4, AG9, AG15). Mail in AG1 pidgeon hole is collected by Asst Chief Clerk AG1 (L/Cpl Collis) and sorted out in the Chief Clerks office. Then he puts it into the trays for AG1(a), AG1(b), AG1(c), AG1(f), and AG1(mp). We then collect it and it finally comes into my in-tray for booking, registering, referencing, filing and ready for the Officer's (Major Parry) action. If an HQ wants to do something, they must get permission first.

I am finishing off this letter over a meat sandwich and a cup of cocoa. Then I will get my KD out of the Dhobi[21] and get between the sheets (I was going to say the sheeps).

---

21 Dhobi = laundry

It is surprising how much we all look forward to getting our battledress off. The material is horrible after the smooth KD We could wear that for ever, it is the best material I have ever worn. I always wore it in preference to civvies for going out. But soon I will be wearing them, when KD is sorrowfully put away for t' winter.

Much love to all,
David

12th November 1948
AG1(b) Branch
GHQ
M.E.L.F.

Dear Mum and Dad,

Last night I got the enlargement of the Highland Herd to ½ plate size. Now everyone is saying what a masterpiece of photography it is. At first they thought I had just bought it and could hardly believe it when I told them what it is. The general impression is that it is a bit of a photographic genius.

I hope you have had an enlargement of it as I don't want to chance losing the negative. But you can be sure I won't lose it.

I also went to the 'flics' last night and saw "Tarzan and the Huntress", as well as Leon Errol in "Twin Husbands", a comedy.

Tomorrow Thursday is a demonstration flight at 5.0pm by a Vampire meteor jet aircraft, which will take off from GHQ Aerodrome, dive towards the C-in-C's building, and then fly low over the waterfront at top speed towards Port Said.

On Saturday is the Derby day Fete, which I think I described in my last letter, and a commentary of the race in England will be broadcast by loud speakers.

Could you send me the negative of "HARLECH CASTLE" and "ABERGLASLYN PASS" as I think these two are worth enlarging. If you don't know which the "ABERGLASLYN PASS" one is, it is the one taken longways and Monty is standing on a rock in the middle of a stream bordered by a forest and backed by a high cliff:

I will write again after the Derby Day Fete and tell you all about it.

Much love to all
David xxx

14th November 1948
AG1(b) Branch
GHQ
M.E.L.F.

Dear Keith,

Very many thanks for your short letter, it only took me two hours to read and translate. As it happens, I am very good at that sort of thing.

I start with a Kenneth and George "Wotcha" same as you, and by using even higher mathematics the time should work out to be 11.45am Eastern time, 10.45am Double British Summer time, and 9.45am Greenwich Mean Time.

Your first paragraph being Top Secret, I will go on to the second which deals with "Sport – New Footy."

The teams which are supported in this tent are Birmingham and Aston Villa (Dick Bradley), Derby Country and Leicester City (Tony Collis), Wrexham and Chester (Taffy Davies), Arsenal and West Ham (Harry Fryer), Liverpool (Me), and Leeds United (Jack Hewitt). Also, Jack Hewitt has a Rugger team, Hunslet.

My team in the sweep was Chesterfield, I still don't know what they got, everyone here is so helpful I still don't even know who won the sweep. Tony Collis came in and let fly some awrful language because Derby got beat for the first time (3-0 by Newcastle).

I just managed to see the first newspaper for four days as the Egyptian Mail and Egyptian Gazette offices and press were blown up in Cairo by someone. Anyway, all the Merseyside teams won except New Brighton which drew with Bradford.

This morning we had a kickaround on the Hockey Pitch which gradually developed into a small game and subsequently to a mad scramble to control the Ball in a very high wind and sandstorm that has been getting stronger since 3am this morning. It has also gone quite cold with this high wind, the temperature dropping to 60°, I have actually had to put a bush-jacket on over my white shirt. The showers this morning were freezing.

Tony Collis has just gone off to the speedway at the Olympia Stadium, he goes every meeting. Taffy isn't interested in anything except demob.

About this choir business, it seems as if it may be falling to pieces, but don't forget to let me know definitely who is to be the new regular choirmaster and if I would like him if I ever go back. All these alterations have put me off it a bit, I may go back in the choir, if it is still a good one, but with Mr Maiden gone it is likely to get *alakeefik*.

Don't try and kid me that Phyllis Evans is nearly 20 because I'm nowhere near 20 myself yet.

I went to the pictures last night to see a rotten picture called "Adventure Island," but there was a good film on about Argentina and for over half the film we were travelling round the high-spots of Buenos Aires (pronounced Buaynos Aeeres), each syllable is pronounced distinctly.

Just as I write this I receive a letter from Mum & Dad enclosing also a letter from Magada which was posted in Pergamino on the 5th November, not bad going.

I have nearly finished my fourth bar of chocolate this weekend, and at the moment it is dead-on 3pm Egyptian time, Sunday 14th November.

I think I will write my next paragraph in French:

Deux femmes qui s'appellent June et Betty sont passées près de cette tente et comme il y a le vent fort les vêtements ne restent pas à bas. Alors tous les soldats près de la rue sont crient à haut voix à ces deux filles.

Comme tu sais, il y a cinq tentes qui sont à dix mètres des chemin, et toujours nous voyons les belles dames passant vers le 'Old Victorians Lido.' Comme il fait très chaud ici elles ne portent pas beaucoup.

In case my French has degenerated muchly and as there is nothing else to say in English, I will finish this letter for now.

Love
David xx

Translation:
Two ladies called June and Betty passed near this tent and as there was a strong wind their clothes did not stay in position down. Then all the soldiers near the street shouted in loud voices at the two girls.

As you know there are five tents ten metres from the street, and we always see the lovely ladies passing towards the 'Old Victorian Lido'. As it is very warm here they weren't wearing much.

16th November 1948
AG1(b) Branch
GHQ
M.E.L.F.

Dear Mum and Dad,

Many thanks for a letter received last Saturday, I think I got about three letters last week, the best yet.

Yesterday, Monday, we knocked off work at 12am (10am GMT) for the day, as Princess Elizabeth had a baby. General Crocker only let us know we were to have the rest of the day off at 11.15am.

On Saturday afternoon the weather changed, and I haven't been warm since. The first phenomena was a high wind which started warm but gradually got cooler, till on the Sunday morning it was freezing, the temperature down to 52°F. On the Sunday morning the wind started to lift the sand, and it did not drop until yesterday morning. Now we have to put three blankets (one doubled) and two sheets on). December and January are the coldest months.

Jack has just said that as soon as he can get some credits to get civvy slacks he will be able to come to Ismailia with me and Tony Collis so it will only be a couple of weeks.

It gets dark now at 5.30pm and is almost daylight at 6am. It is not long now before the shortest day (the same here as in England).

Tony Collis is just trying to mend the floor of the tent on the edge where his bed is, he got a hammer and hit the slab of concrete in the middle. Instead of going into place it broke into five pieces and he is now trying to fit it together.

To illustrate the language of the Army, Jack just got up and said "Shut the *** door of this *** tent, *** wind is as cold as *** ice."

The picture tonight is another rotten one called "Union Pacific," a cowboy, horrible.

There was a rumour that the top-secret release programme is in SMC (Staff Message Control) and we should therefore know in about 10 days time. December 14th is the date for the restart of demob.

The lights have just gone out in all the tents, the cookhouse, and the NAAFI. So, as usual, I am the one that has everything, out come three candles and I start to write again. Tony is fed up and blowing away on his mouth again, trying to get someone to join in. But unless I am there there is never a sing-song in the tent.

Good King Wenceslas, *Hark the Herald Angels Sing*, *Once in Royal Davids City*, *Oh Come all ye Faithful*, I have managed to get all these heathens interested in carols, in fact, I think they really like them. I will be called a Missionary next.

Supper was quite good tonight, I had four meat pasties, potatoes, and peas, as well as some rice pudding. The blokes serving couldn't see what they were giving out so we got a bit more than usual.

Well, the other candles have been extinguished and mine is to be the next, so goodnight.

Much love to all,
David

8th December 1948
AG1(b) Branch
GHQ
M.E.L.F.

Dear Mum & Dad

This morning we had a new clerk in the office. We call him Steve, his release group is 139 and he comes from Walthamstow, London. He is quiet and not common, when he told me his group, I told myself, "This is where I become an old soldier." I felt quite chuffed when I said that I was the next one out of the office to go on demob, next July or August, and that when Bill Dillon does on Python next October he should move up a lot. Its a lot of luck really.

Whereas I have been trying to get warm over the stove early this morning, Steve said he was hot. So for goodness sake have a fire when I come home.

When I first came out here, my group was high, now it is quite low. Just think that if they had not stopped release, 105 group would have gone home on demob by now, and 106 would be almost going. I am the first to go on demob out of out office.

I have just heard that G.H.Q will probably dissolve into a high policy unit next March. Naturally the establishment will be cut down and it is thought that some may go to East Africa, and some to HQ BTE which is to take over. By then I will be too low a group to be moved, so I should stay with G.H.Q. dealing with high policy correspondence.

I am going to the pictures tonight to see "Dark Journey," a German spy film.

Having now seen the film I have come to the conclusion that it was no good. When we got outside the Cameronia, it was freezing cold, being 8-30pm, and we dashed back to the tent. I think the temperature drops to as low as 45° at evening and just before dawn to 35°. Last year the abnormal temperature of 30° was recorded at Cairo.

Many thanks for yet another parcel of magazines and newspapers. The magazines come in useful even when I have finished with them as then they go round the tent. The papers always have interesting news in them.

There is no other news from here.

Christmas might easily be six months away instead of two weeks. Our holidays are now official, viz: from Thursday 23rd at 13.15 till Tuesday 28th at 08.30.

Is Dad's place as generous?

Of course there'll be tons and tons of work, but that will probably make time fly when we get back.

Don't forget to let me have a long narrative after Christmas of everything that happened, from all points of view. But I will write again this weekend.

Much love to all
David xxx

December 1948
AG1(b) Branch
GHQ
M.E.L.F.

Dear Mum & Dad,

Many thanks for your letter which I received yesterday evening (Wed). It is probably one of the quickest I have received.

Well, I was rather surprised to read that Monty called, but not that he was a sergeant as you can't really help it in the (????).

Smoking is alright in the Army as there is a free issue of 50 a week and cigarettes cost 6d for 20. But when we get into Civilian life again it would almost drive you crackers. That is why I don't smoke.

Let me know if I have time to write to him at his home address or if it would be better to write to his unit (72 F.S.S. BAOR 11).

It seems that all the others are abroad now, and I should think that, next to Monty, I am the best off. Don't forget, Ernie went as a gunman in the Royal Artillery, Gordon Bibby as a clerk in the R.A.O.C. etc.

And all those that went in for a commission have failed by the looks of it. Still it's hopeless thinking that the Army will give you a commision when you have such a short time to serve.

Out here the weather is cooling off very very slightly and it is quite bearable.

The only time I sweat is when I drink tea or coffee indoors, or after any exertion (eg walking fast or rushing about). It is actually quite cold in the mornings. We have also been getting some clouds lately.

On the 30th of this month there is to be a big change in the billeting of personnel.

At present there are 4 coys 1, 2, 3, and 4. I am in 3 company, the proposal is to billet personnel by their Branches. All "G" branch and auxiliary Branches will go into 4 company. "AG" "Pay" "Medical" "Welfare" "Education" "Intelligence" and auxiliaries into 3 Coy, (so I stay where I am), ST and "Q" Branch into 2 Coy, and C-in-C, MGA, MS, etc. into 1 Coy.

I have just come back from the Pictures where I saw "Action for Slander," pretty good film.

Well, that seems to be all the latest news, except that all towns and cities in Egypt are now inbounds to British Troops, (CAIRO and ALEXANDRIA when in civilian clothes).

Much love to all
David xxx

December 1948
AG1(b) Branch
GHQ
M.E.L.F.

1. Of what are Ayrshire, Guernsey and Longhorn types?
2. Who is the here in Dickens' Pickwick Papers?
3. What form of government has Brazil?
4. When was Tunney's last fight?
5. What month in the year has the longest name?
6. Which country raises most of the world's tobacco?
7. In English, which vowel is used most?
8. India & Afghanistan are connected by what pass?
9. Which was the only tree that was forbidden in the Garden of Eden
10. Benares is the Holy City of what country?
11. Who said: "it is much easier to be critical than to be correct?"
12. Name the four principal divisions of the brain?
13. When is "Groundhog Day"?
14. How many beats are there to a measure in Waltz time?
15. What woman of Greek mythology had bronze claws and hair composed of serpents?
16. In mathematics what is the limit of the greatest assignable number?
17. Which is the second smallest continent?
18. What cigarette advertises "something new added"?
19. What is the length of life of a house fly?
20. What singers succeeded the Minnesingers in Germany?
21. Did London Bridge ever fall down?
22. Is the capital of Egypt Alexandria or Cairo?
23. What is the English title of "Adeste Fideles"?

24. Name the five things King Cole wanted?
25. If it takes a man a week to walk a fortnight, how many apples are there in a barrel of pears?
26. Where were the Olympics held in 1936?
27. Where is the world's largest bridge?
28. A limousine and an old Ford leave town at 3pm. The limousine goes east at 40mph and breaks down at 4pm. The Ford travels west at 20mph, how far apart will they be at 5.30pm?
29. What popular sport was popularly an amateur sport till 1926?
30. Are bats blind?

Answers:
1. Cows
2. Mr Pickwick
3. Republic
4. 1928
5. September
6. USA
7. E
8. Khyber Pass
9. Tree of Knowledge of God & Evil
10. India
11. Benjamin Disraeli
12. Cerebrum, Cerebullum, Pons Varolii and Medulla Oblongata
13. Feb 2nd
14. 3
15. Medusa
16. Infinity
17. Europe
18. Old Gold
19. 8-10 weeks
20. The Meistersingers
21. Yes, by storm in 1091
22. Cairo
23. Come all ye faithful
24. His pipe, bowl and three fiddlers
25. None
26. Berlin
27. Oakland, San Francisco
28. 90 miles
29. Tennis
30. No

2nd January 1949
AG1(b) Branch
GHQ
M.E.L.F.

Dear Mum & Dad,

This is my first New Year letter; so here goes.

I got up this morning at midday after sleeping from 10pm to 10am this morning which means that I missed breakfast and even missed the NAAFI. But you know how many times I used to get up at 10am and nearly always missed breakfast at home in an effort to be in time for choir. I believe that whatever happens at the beginning of the year happens throughout the year.

A while ago, I think you recommended me to see the film "Spring in Park Lane" with Anna Neagle & Mike Wilding. So – I saw it last night at the Cameronia I thought it was one of the best of his films.

Many thanks for Dad's letter which I received yesterday, New Years Day. I see that I should [x] another letter tomorrow.

The day before yesterday at approximately 11.10am, exactly a year after leaving Lime Street, I got a letter from – Phyllis! So, I suppose that's another letter to write.

Up at work I have been Chief Clerk for the last two days as Bill Dillon has been absent, and as far as I know, I am doing the job O.K. Steve is still in the office, and Vick has had his posting to the Sudan postponed.

The weather has been quite cold lately, even during the day, on the average temperature has been about 60 degrees during the day and out of the wind. We will all be glad when we go back into K.D for two reasons: one is that it is much better than battledress, smoother, cleaner and easier to put on, the other is that when we change, we shall know that the next time we shall change back into B.D. will be on the journey home. Usually, the change takes place at Gibraltar, but on the Medloc route, the change is at Trieste or Toulon am the French Riviera.

While I have been writing this letter, Harry has just triumphantly state that he has written 30 pages of letters. But all his material is about Alexandria. As he knew someone there, he had a good time, because that is where he stayed.

Well, I get the films tomorrow night so I will send an envelope with them in on Tuesday morning. There are 13 snaps altogether, all are of some person or persons.

Now that everyone is getting over the effects of Christmas we have to start looking forward to the new release programme and the Easter.

Jack has just brought a pile of magazines and books which he said originated in West Kirby, so I think I will finish and read them before tea and then off to the pictures again to see "A man about the house."

Much love to all
David xx

2nd February 1949
AG1(b) Branch
GHQ
M.E.L.F.

Dear Mum & Dad,

Very many thanks for your letter containing a Christmas card from Magada.

In my next letter but one, I will be sending the snaps, as they will be ready on Friday & I will be writing over the weekend. (That sound like my next letter as it is Wednesday already. At the end of this letter is a list of the snaps as I have taken them (16).

This morning a civilian came into the office and managed to stumble out the words "Open door, hut 70", which meant nothing at all to us, he couldn't understand us when we asked him questions. So of course, I twigged it straight away and came to the rescue.

I knew he was French somehow and you should have seen his face when I spoke to him in French, he beamed all over and started rattling away so fast that at it took me all my time & concentration to keep up with him, but I did it.

Quite a number of people have come in with queries in French etc lately.

78 Group, 79 Group and 101 Group are all going on release on Sunday. And so, the 100 groups start. Just think if they hadn't deferred release for three months from the 14th September till the 14th December, Group 108 would have gone on demob. Only 10 more groups to go, and I would definitely been home in July (beginning). I will definitely be demobbed at Aldershot.

I read in the papers yesterday that woolen cloth is now off coupons in Britain and I suppose that means woolen goods as well. But I still don't vote for the Labour government next year, you never know what they're going to do next. This is only a move to try to get in again in 1950. I know *I* won't vote for them.

This time last year I had just passed Cape Bon, which is in Tunisia, North Africa. I remember it as a massive rocky headland, very barren and steep. We could see quite a lot as we were only about ten miles out.

Then tomorrow, the 3rd February we called at Malta and saw the Mediterranean fleet.

This morning we had a signal in saying that mail posted on 28th and 29th January in England has been considerably held up as the planes have been grounded owing to severe fog.

Well, I must finish there, so…

Much love to all,
David xxx

February 1949
AG1(b) Branch
GHQ
M.E.L.F.

Dear Mum and Dad,

This is just a short note to state the sock situation. They're getting worn now and I won't be able to get them changed for a while.

It is possible to send socks out, so what is wanted is a good pair of woolen socks (fairly thick), so that they can stand the heat. All I'm hoping is that they're not rationed at home. The socks we buy out here are hopeless being made with Egyptian, and in this climate they must be wool as wool itself is thick and stronger than cotton.

All my other clothes are in good condition, and once we go into KD. I won't have to wear them any more, not even the smallest stitch except KD shirt and slacks. At the rate the weather is going we will be going into KD at the end of march, and permanently from the middle of April.

The two towels are as good as new, that is, since I just got them at Chester.

The neck of one of my three shirts has frayed, but two shirts are easily sufficient. I've got good ties.

I never have to wear underclothes, so they're as good as new. As for shoes, I'm well away, two good pairs, and when they're worn, it takes only 24 hours to get them repaired.

And so socks seem to be the only trouble, so I hope you can fish out a pair for me.

Much love to all,
David

February 1949
AG1(b) Branch
GHQ
M.E.L.F.

Dear Mum and Dad,

It is now exactly one year since I walked into AG1(b) and started work. At that time s/sgt Ranson was Chief Clerk of AG1(b), and Jim Walker was Chief Clerk AG1(a), which was in the room then. I never thought that at the same time next year I would be Chief Clerk of AG1(b).

I have received four parcels of newspapers this week and one letter, for which, many thanks. In one of the parcels was the Caronia supplement which I will digest today.

On Friday morning I went in to see Maj Parry about the job as I wanted to know why I didn't seem to be getting anywhere, being in the office for exactly a year, and being a Class 2 Clerk since May. he said that I am doing very well as Chief Clerk and that he has been considering my promotion.

He also said that at the end of the month he will call me in and let me know if I am keeping up the same standard or have even improved, which probably means that if I have improved he will make me a sergeant or if I am still the same, a corporal.

But I still can't see why I am not a full corporal yet, as everywhere outside AG they usually get paid for the job they are doing. Still, this is AG Branch, where there are hardly any Sergeants.

However, I have the consolation that I am successful which will count a lot in civvy street. And I am only in the Army till August.

Latest demob news is that the shipping programme goes up to April, and that 104 group is going on Friday, (not Tuesday). 105 will be going a week next Sunday.

Last night at the pictures we saw "Against the Wind!" with Jack Warner – a spy film.

The weather has warmed up a bit today, as last week it was very bad, cold, windy, and plenty of rain. I think they are collecting the stoves in on Thursday whether it is cold or not.

Capt. Danby wanted to know when I was going to take some leave, so I thought of taking some just after we go into KD. The two alternatives I have now thought of are Seaview, or Troodos Holiday Camp, Cyprus. I can only go to Cyprus if I get a fortnight, which isn't likely. Alexandria is too big and "lonely" for a decent leave so I have heard. I can go to Cairo on one of the weekend outings from here. And Luxor is too dear (£9), excluding fare. I have been to Suez and Tinusa, so if I can't get a fortnight's leave, it will have to be Port Said again. But I had a damn good time there last time, which is what you want really.

I have had a letter from the Rector and one from Val giving me all the latest outside information, and I see that Ron Fallon had his 21st Birthday a couple of weeks ago and was presented with 27/6d from the club to buy a medical scarf, whatever that is. I also hear that the choir has improved 100% since about a week after Mr Maiden went, as it collapsed completely when he did go. Lastly, Pat Taylor is engaged!

Do you intend to keep the dog or not, now that it has worms and seems to be a bit of a devil?

Also ask Keith for another list of members of the choir. The rector seems quite keen to see me back.

I still have a couple of letters to write so I might as well rush through them before tea.

Much love to all,
David

13th February 1949
AG1(b) Branch
GHQ
M.E.L.F.

Dear Mum and Dad,

Very many thanks for the letter and 5/- book of stamps. They will, of course, come in very useful. I also received a very nice letter from the Rector at the same time so I will be replying to that today.

I have taken the negatives back to get some more prints, so they will be ready by Tuesday. You should have received the first few snaps by now, and I hope you are keeping the negatives and snaps by for my album. I can't really keep one out here so bit by bit I will send most of the ones I don't want home. I will be keeping one or two negatives that I might need, you know what I mean.

I noticed that in the sheet of the News Chronicle, every article was about Liverpool. And talking about Liverpool I notice they are out of the cup, being beaten 3-1 by Wolves. New Brighton were also beaten by Mansfield, and Tranmere drew.

For three weeks the weather here has been very bad, cold, high winds and gales, and most surprising thing of all, plenty of rain. One night last week it was so bad that the lights were off for two days. I am enclosing a cutting from the Egyptian Gazette.

This time last year I was at BTD, Suez, and for some queer reason demob seems just as far away now as it did then, but if I was to think this time last year that I would be going home about August, I suppose I would have gone mad.

The latest demob grif (?) is that 102 group are going tomorrow, 103 are going *page ends, missing following pages*

Index to films:

1. From Bridge over Sweetwater Canal, between Camp and the Lido Stadium.
2. View in the wog village
3. Palm trees and typical shop
4. View from Treaty Road (Port Said – Suez)
5. In camp

Much love to all,
David

27th February 1949
AG1(b) Branch
GHQ
M.E.L.F.

Dear Mum and Dad,

For at least one week I am to be Chief Clerk of AG1(b) and AG(c), as Mary Hodge is going on leave.

Another thing is that I have heard Maj Parry has been into the Chief Clerk's office asking for a promotion proforma, but whether anything will become of it or not, I don't know. Everyone is remarking how unlucky I am to have such "tight" officers, and everyone in AG1 hates him. At least two people have said that the section is going better now than before Christmas. Mr Green, a WO and Chief Clerk of AG4 says it's ridiculous for a L/Cpl to do the job I'm doing.

But every week that passes is a week nearer demob.

Group 105 seems to be going on 8th March now, on the ASCANIUS, but I don't know the English port. After discussions and talks and… knows what I think I should leave here about the end of August. But in any case 10th October still stands as the latest possible date of release.

The weather has gone slightly warmer, the temperature rising to about 68°F. It has been very cold up to now, yet the blokes who have just come out from England seem to think it is quite warm. In April we change into KD, thank goodness, and when I take this BD off I know that the next time I shall ever put it on is on release, or really that I shall never wear it again.

The picture at the Cameronia tonight is "The Noose Hangs High" with Bud Abbott and Lou Costello. The others say it isn't much good, but I think I'll go just the same.

Mary Stewart is getting married on 5th March, and I will probably be going to the Service. Brad says he's getting engaged when he is demobbed.

On Thursday we have the first cross "country?" run, and everyone is groaning etc. I remember at Chester (the last time), I came 22nd out of over 300 runners, and 4th, 3rd and 2nd respectively in the three trial runs.

I didn't go to the pictures after all, so in a few minutes we will be going for supper in the cookhouse, it will be my first time for five months.

So I'll finish this short letter here.

Much love to all,
David

28th February 1949
AG1(b) Branch
GHQ
M.E.L.F.

Dear Mum and Dad,

It is now almost March and I have six months to go (from what I have heard).

On Friday evening all the women came to work in civvies as they had been to Sally Peters' wedding in the afternoon, and what a row they made, some of them had just drunk enough to be merry.

Now Mary Stewart has gone on three weeks leave to get married. If you ask me, it's just stupid, and out here!

On 1st April, we have an English civilian coming to work here, and from what I hear, she either lives in Wallasey or has some connection with it. Martin Powell from SWOAG's office told me that yesterday.

Tonight we are going to the pictures to see "Easy Money", with Jack Warner. It is about five people who each win about £57,000 on the football pools.

Then next Sunday Ivy Benson will be back at the GHQ theatre, so we may go again.

The weather is still cold with occasional heavy gusts of wind and heavy skies. We will probably go into KD now about 19th April, which means that the periods for BD and KD are six months each. We are in Battledress longer than I thought. But it is probably better as going back to England I would practically freeze, even at the middle of summer.

Further information about the civvy reveals that her mother comes from Wallasey.

Many thanks to Keith for his letter which I have just received. What I want now is a diagram of the positions in the choir. Is Mr Jones (Tenor), still there?

The latest rumours about demob are that 116, 117, and 118 groups are leaving here together at the end of July, and the general opinion is that 118 will leave at the end of July or beginning of August. This seems to leave me with five months to do, as I consider myself demobbed when I leave here.

The last two days, there has been tons of work in the office and I am just managing to keep it under control, so if I don't get another stripe (?) after this, I never will. But I've got a feeling I will (This pen seems to be conking out now, I've had it 14 months).

Paddy's going up to the Branch now and he will probably be bringing down some mail, so I hope to get a letter. Keith's is the only one I've had in the last ten days.

Paddy McGuigan is an Irish Regular going on demob in June to Belfast, I know him very well.

Jack Hewitt is going on the "Ascanius" on 8th March, and not the "Emperor." It is going to Liverpool.

Well, I think I may as well finish now, I have been writing this letter all afternoon.

Much love to all,
David

6th March 1949
AG1(b) Branch
GHQ
M.E.L.F.

Dear Mum and Dad,

Note the change, I am promoted a P/A/Cpl with effect from 1st Feb '49, which means that all back money for a Corporal's pay goes into credits.

Everyone is saying that it was about Parry did something. The next step is a sergeant, but I am not keen on that here until about July.

The pay of a 3 star Corporal (me) is 9/6d a day, compared with 4/- when I started. Of that 6d a day goes for Insurance, 1/- a day voluntary allotment, and 4½d for something else, but the 4½d is counteracted by clothing allowance, so I am entitled to draw 56/- per week. I actually draw 30/-.

I was £21-14-9 in credit as at 18 Feb '49. At the moment I should be £25 in credit according to my own reckoning, but the Army Paymaster may think different. I haven't drawn any since I came in, so it shouldn't be far wrong.

Yesterday 104 and 105 groups went Home on demob, so I am now group no: 13. When I just came I was group no: 30.

The weather is still the same, fairly warm, calm, very few clouds. We should be in KD by Easter, so time should then go quicker till July, then I can start to get ready. I should know my release dates this month, so I will let you know when as soon as possible.

Many thanks for Mum's letter and Magada's which was enclosed. I received it half an hour ago.

I am glad you may be able to do something about socks, Brad (my friend) says that it is possible to send socks through the post.

I should think they would be personal effects.

I am continuing in pencil as I have just got into bed and I can't remember where I have put my pen.

We have just come back the pictures after seeing "Miranda," a film very out of the ordinary and very funny, not jokes, but the situation. Glynis Johns is the Mermaid and David Tomlinson is also one of the main stars.

Tomorrow is "Sleeping Car to Trieste" which you mentioned in your letter.

I am now at work Monday morning so seeing that I can't carry on at the moment I will continue tomorrow.

Much love to all,
David

20th March 1949
AG1(b) Branch
GHQ
M.E.L.F.

Dear Mum and Dad,

Well, at last I can give you my exact release dates. They are: 9th Sep 49 till 19th Sep 49

These are the dates between which I will be released at Aldershot, England.

So it looks as if I will probably arrive Home exactly two years after I left to join at Chester on 18th Sep 49.

I should leave GHQ at the latest by 1st September, so I like to think of 31st July as the end as during August I will be handing over the job and cleaning up in general.

That gives me 133 days to go.

The War Office signal came into our office on Thursday and I was one of the first out of the hundreds of people in GHQ to know, and what's more I was one of the only people in GHQ who were supposed to know. I had the big job of redrafting it, typing on a stencil, and summing (?) it off. Then I had to despatch it to Commands and to all persons in GHQ not below the rank of Brigadier. It was a hush-hush job.

There is a rumour that the new civilian typist is coming into AG1 tomorrow, Monday. She is the one I told you of, and who probably comes from Wallasey, in any case, her mother definitely lives in Wallasey.

The weather is warming up considerably in the last few days, yesterday it was about 70°F in the shade.

The rain and winds have gone and we hope to go into KD in a few weeks. All those who haven't got KD have been measured, so they should get it next week which is usually about two weeks before we actually go into it. The stoves have all been collected.

Last night at the Cameronia we saw "Killer McCoy" with Mickey Rooney. It was the first time I have been to the pictures this week as I have had so much to do.

It started off with Monday, a full working day, and what time we have off in the afternoon isn't much.

On Tuesday I was 2 i/c Guard in GHq, which starts at 2.15pm.

Then on Wednesday morning work again, rushed back over for dinner. After dinner I had to change into football kit to play for AG against G (?) Branch. They won 4-2. I was playing outside right.

Work again at 4pm till 8pm.

On Thursday, work in the morning and the Release Programme to despatch etc: I got back at 2pm. I had to be down at the Olympia stadium (one mile away) by 2.30pm as I was in the sports (long jump and discus). I didn't get back till 5pm, so it was too late to do anything then.

Friday was a full working day with pay, which took up the whole afternoon.

Saturday morning was work again and for about two hours in the afternoon there were a lot of personal things to see to which I never had time to during the week. So after that I have been free.

Till tomorrow, when there is P.T. in the morning, and TAB inoculations in the afternoon, besides being a full working day.

But I think that Tuesday will be free and then the rest of the week.

A week on Friday is 1st April. And then Easter arrives. That is a holiday, and I will put in for some leave as soon as possible after that, and then start looking forward.

Many thanks for Dad's letter which I received on Thursday at 8.30am, but which I never had time to read till 5pm.

If Dad is definitely going to London I will give him a small lecture on what to expect.

The flies are coming again and show signs of becoming a b**** nuisance before the week is out.

So I will finish this letter for today, as there is nothing else to say but chocolate to eat.

Much love to all,
David

22nd March 1949
AG1(b) Branch
GHQ
M.E.L.F.

Dear Mum & Dad,

At the moment I am lying on bed with a pair of gym pants on trying to keep cool as the weather has gone HOT all of a sudden.

It started last night about midnight when the wind got up and increased in intensity getting hotter every minute. I woke up this morning for about the 6th time covered in sand, it had got in everywhere. So, all morning there has been a scorching hot wind blowing and sweat has been pouring off us. They all say that one feels the 2nd Egyptian summer worse than the first.

106 Group went on demob this morning and at the height of the sandstorm (about 3am).

On Saturday, 107 Group is going and 108 is leaving at the beginning of April in just over a fortnights time. Then it will be group no 10.

Tomorrow Vera Pearson comes under AGI (b) while Maj Wallis (her boss) is in East Africa. Up till now she has been on leave and "Ginger" Maggs has been in charge of the section (which is AG9). Tomorrow when Vera comes back, he goes on leave and Maj Parry takes over AG9.

She is a sergeant in the ATS, while he, the assistant, is only a Private.

As I have said before, after Easter 15th-18th April, I will out in for some leave as soon as possible and after that start looking forward.

I am wondering whether to get a bike of some sort when I get home as I may go on a couple of day rides or one or two rides when I stay over somewhere, for instance, Anglesey.

Mary Stewart is being demobbed locally tomorrow as she was married a couple of weeks ago on the 5th March. There seems to be no immediate replacement.

Mary Hodge is now, therefore, the only one left in AGI(c) & she will be leaving next month.

Last night AGI(b) was on the wireless. John O'Neill had a "request from Home" played, and it was "In the Monastery Garden" Imagine, *my* section on the wireless.

Many thanks for your letter which I received this morning.

Well, the only one of us who seems to be doing well is Monty and it looks as if I have come second. But I still maintain that it is a lot of luck.

As for the one or two women you mentioned, as far as I'm concerned you can keep 'em, because they can't have much sense. When I get back, I have a darn site (sic) more important things to do. For one thing I want to make sure that my Army credits go to good use.

Tonight, I must go to the pictures for the first time this week. So, I will get a wash & put this letter in its envelope.

Much love to all,
David xxx

3rd April 1949
AG1(b) Branch
GHQ
M.E.L.F.

Dear Mum and Dad,

Very many thanks for two letters on Friday, one from Keith.

April is here, and it is May next month. As I have said before I should arrive home on 18th September, but the actual date I am looking forward to as the end of the Army is 31st July. then, of course, I will be handing over the job and packing up in general as I am leaving at the end of August.

Easter Holidays are now official, and they are from 1.15pm Thursday 14th 'til 8.15am on Tuesday 19th. That gives us four clear days and I am not yet decided what to do with them yet.

Then I get the Saturday following Easter weekend off.

Leave has again been postponed indefinitely, probably till the end of June as going out of camp on leave has lately become a very awkward business, with regard to kit.

With effect from tomorrow we can wear KD in the daytime IF WE WANT TO. Did you ever hear of the Army doing a thing like that?

Anyway, as it is still rather cool in the early morning I will be wearing BD for another week, and so will everyone else.

I have seen a photo in the paper of Piccadilly Circus with all the lights on, and I suppose it will be the same in Liverpool.

I see the Wolves are playing Leicester City in the cup final at Wembley sometime in May. some of the chaps here want to know if Keith went to Everton to see the replay, and if so, they want a full report.

At work there is nothing much doing except that Mary is going at the end of this month, and there is no replacement as yet. Capt. Leather is coming back off leave on 6th April (after a month), and Major Wallis is coming back from East Africa on 11th, so we relinquish Command of AG9 then.

I have no comments to make on Keith's letter except that the football teams must be extremely short of men, and the same applies to the girls.

It seems that the British weather is catching up on us out here, but once we get going we will leave your temperature standing. It is warm during the day now at 80°F and it has still to go very warm, hot, and very hot, which is approx.126°F.

107 group is going on Tuesday so I will then be group no 10, with 168 days to demob, and 119 days to 31st July.

How is the sock situation, can you send a pair out? If you've got a pair to spare, I could do with them, especially when we go into KD I won't be able to wear shorts until I get a pair of long ones. Don't forget, they come as personal effects.

It is almost dinnertime, so if I can think of anything to write this afternoon, I will put it in.

Well, there wasn't anything and Brad is waiting to post this letter, so I will finish.

Much love to all,
David

7th April 1949
AG1(b) Branch
GHQ
M.E.L.F.

Dear Mum and Dad,

Many thanks for the papers and magazines, which I received yesterday (Wednesday).

There was one article in the "Post" about the 'Homely Club', Canal South District, M.E.L.F. Well, that is our MMG Canteen by the Cameronia.

The picture at the Cameronia tonight is "The Invisible Man Returns" original story by H.G.Wells.

I don't know if I have told you before, but Major Read has gone home to England on PYTHON, which is leave for Regular officers and en. They have to do a period of three years overseas before they are due for it.

Major Parry is taking over the section now, so we are composed of three officers:

- MAJ PARRY (DAAG)
- Capt O'HAGAN (S/Capt)
- Capt LEATHER (S/Capt)

and three Clerks:

- S/Sgt SCOTT (Chief Clerk)
- Cpl DILLON (Release Clerk)
- Me (Policy and Conditions of Service Clerk)

Of these, Capt O'Hagan is being posted to CYRENAICA, and S/Sgt Scott is going on release (75 Group, DOV).

Continued 8th April 1949

It is Friday now (payday), and the picture last night was alright, and very "spooky!"

The time is now almost 8.15 and we are 'supposed' to start work, whether we do or not is a different matter as we don't get much in these days.

As Bill Dillon is in hospital I have to do both the Release and Conditions of Service sides, and there is a lot more to it now than mere films and getting a letter ready for action by the Officers. But I can do it alright.

Before I finish, I would just like to remind you about the negatives if there are any to be found.

Much love to all,
David

10th April 1949
AG1(b) Branch
GHQ
M.E.L.F.

Dear Mum and Dad,

Many thanks for your letter and also one from Keith. I am glad to see that my socks are on the way. I am being pestered by flies here so my writing may be a bit spidery.

At 7.30pm I am going with Johnny O'Neill to the Fayid Education Centre to hear Margaret Lockhart, the Scottish Violinist. We are going to the MMG just to get a supper, four eggs, a plate of chips and (?).

Today has been a real scorcher and tomorrow we are going into KD by day and BD by night. Next weekend, of course, is Easter, and on 2nd May I say goodbye to the Army Battledress for good (until I get to England).

Last night we saw "Here come the Huggetts," the Jack Warner and Kathleen Harrison crowd were in it. I think you have seen it.

Mary Hodge is finishing work on Thursday at 1.15pm, as she is taking a fortnights leave straight after Easter and then is going on 6th May on the Emperor of Australia, docking at Liverpool. She has asked me to write to her address in Cornwall which is Trevisquite, St Mabyn, Cornwall.

If it is any help to you, it is near Wadebridge, just inland from the rocky west coast.

The weather is still undecided as it will be very warm one day and cooler the next. April should see more consistent weather, and it is, of course, the month for KD thank goodness.

I was talking to a chap today who had been across Medloc route four times, and he said the exact route was from Trieste to

Milan, and then across the Austrian Tyrol to the Rhine Valley, and ended at Hook of Holland. We still live in hopes that we may go that way.

I have worked out that from 23rd April, if you regard it as the day I joined up, 18th Sep '47 to 31st August, the approximate date of embarkation home, is the same period of time as till the date of embarkation for Port Said.

We have now got new hours at GHQ. start at 08.00 (8-o-clock), and finish at 13.15 (1.15pm). But at night time for three times a week we start at 5pm, and finish at 7.30pm instead of 8pm. Also you are allowed one Saturday off per month.

After I get home I must go down to Johnny O'Niell's house in Widnes as he wants me to go.

His address is 71, Irwell Street, Widnes, Lancs. It is 15 miles from the Pier Head, not as far as Chester.

By the way, has Pat responded to the request for pin-ups yet?

Well, I can't think of anything else for tonight. I will write again before the week is out.

Much love to all,
David

April 1949
AG1(b) Branch
GHQ
M.E.L.F.

Dear Mum and Dad,

Very many thanks for your letter which I received last Friday. Well, you certainly did have a very lucky week, and you can be sure that I will be looking forward to trying on that sports jacket that was sent.

I will be writing to Keith this weekend, it happens to be a holiday for us (Monday). Evesham is mainly a fruit region so most of the time he should be picking fruit, or rather, eating it. It is one of the few places I have not been to in England, but it is mainly just normal English scenery.

By the way, the camp I am going to is Seaview Holiday Camp, Port Fouad is on the other side of the River Suez from Port Said, I am going next Saturday, but write to GHQ just the same. The camp is run by NAAFI.

On Sunday morning there was great excitement in the camp, a whole row of tents, A1 to A10, were burgled, I am in A6, but you can be sure that I lost nothing as I have enough sense to take the precaution of hiding away all valuables before I go to sleep.

Pete lost 70 piastres (15/-), which was in his paybook in the pocket of his KD shirt which was hanging up.

Ray lost 75 piastres, fountain pen and pencil, 50 cigs, cigarette ticket, comb, and a £1 cigarette case.

There was absolutely nothing at all in my pockets, and I think the bloke was so disgusted that he threw it in a heap by the door.

Ted and "Ginger" Cauldwell are still at Timsa, but two days ago Ginger had his watch stolen.

I don't even put anything under my pillow as it is too obvious I think. Anyway a bloke from the next tent had 60 piastres taken from his wallet which was under his pillow. The wallet was put back.

It is a general opinion that a Britisher did it. All wogs are searched by the SIB[22] before entering or leaving camp.

On Saturday night the film was "Fame is the spur". Tonight, it is "Singapore," and next Sunday, it is "Odd man Out."

Here is a little account of an experience in the study of reptile life which we, (Ray, Pete and Myself), had yesterday morning.

I was reading a book called "KIPPS" by H.G. Wells, when I saw something long streak across the entrance to the tent. On dashing outside I saw it was a lizard very long and narrow, I was able to chase it for a while, until Ray came running up with a cigarette tin. We managed to catch it when it has stopped for a breather. We went back to the tent triumphant with our capture. Pete had a queer idea it was a 'Chameleon' (reptile that changes colour), so he brought in green leaves, khaki socks, and all sorts of queer things, and finally said, "I wonder why it doesn't change colour?" So I pointed out the very simple reason that it probably wasn't a 'Chameleon'.

Anyway, the next idea was to feed it, (we had given it the freedom of a large tin bowl with sides riding sheer for 9".

We half-killed a fly and put it in the bowl, all of a sudden, the lizard's mouth flashed and the fly vanished head-first into the lizard. Ray said "Phew!", Pete said "Crikey!" and I said "Flip!" Anyway, we let it out after feeding it with more flies which it ate heartily. I think it did very well from its short sojourn in the bowl, don't you?

Sunday night the orchestral concert was by Verdi, Rachmaninov, and Sibelius. So I didn't go.

---

22 SIB = Special Investigations Branch of the Royal Military Police

I see Ken is going in the R.A.F. I'm afraid he is going in rather late, as those people who enlist after January 1st 1949 must do five years on the reserve after being demobbed, which, in my opinion, is worse than being in the army for two years. They have nights in the week, and Sunday Parades. Fortunately, I miss all this, so that when I am demobbed I am absolutely free.

Well, I think I will go for a swim and then write to Keith.

Much love to all (three of you)
David

18th April 1949
AG1(b) Branch
GHQ
M.E.L.F.

Dear Mum and Dad,

Easter is almost over now, and it is 1st May a week on Sunday.

I didn't do much over Easter. On the Thursday night we went to see Danny Kaye in "The Secret Life of Walter Mitty," which was so good that they scrapped the film for Friday and Saturday, (The Hairy Ape), and continued with Danny Kaye. besides the numerous requests for an extension there was a full house every night.

On Friday night we went to the Fayid Education Centre and heard parts 1 and 2 of "The Messiah," but it was rather blurred, coming over a loud speaker. The recording was the one of Thomas Beecham with the BBC Orchestra and Choir, nowhere near as good as that by the Liverpool Philharmonic Orchestra and the Huddersfield Choral Society conducted by Sir Malcolm Sergeant.

On Saturday night we went to the MMG to hear it, and that was worse. It was the same recording, but there was a wog working the machine and he never started the record at the beginning, he kept fooling around with the sound so that we could hardly hear it at times. Then the room was packed out and it was sweltering hot, there was a continual noise from outside, and there was discussion as to whether the Hallelujah Chorus or I know that my Redeemer liveth should come first. If anyone was stupid it was that crowd in there. The Hallelujah Chorus is the end of Part 2, and I know that my Redeemer Liveth is the beginning of Part 3, and they didn't know that.

Otherwise we have just been fooling around in general

The weather has been rather cool except yesterday when it got rather hot about midday. I see there was a heat wave in Britain.

Many thanks for the papers which including the supplement of the opening of the new Waterloo Dock. Also a letter from Mum received on Wednesday morning.

A few minutes ago Harry was writing a letter and he asked me how to spell "Thought". He suggested "fort," as being a Londoner he pronounces "th" as "f" invariably.

Another word he always mixes up is "teach" and "learn." In fact I have never heard him use the word "teach", (I'll learn you).

Mary Hodge finished work last Thursday, so that leaves me temporarily in control of two sections, AG1(b) and AG1(c).

After 23rd April I have to do senior NCO[23] duties up at the Branch, that is, duties of sergeants and above.

I think the socks will just arrive in time for the hot weather which should start without a break at the beginning of May.

I see that 18th September is a Sunday. If possible, I want a week on a farm about a week after I get back, I will be getting 24 days leave.

In a weeks time it will be three months to the beginning of August, not long really.

page seems to be missing, next page begins mid-way through sentence

...on Friday 18th Feb, 104 I am not sure about, and 105 should be going on the Empress of Australia on 6th March, due in at Liverpool on 16th March. I noticed on that News Chronicle sheet that the propellers of the OTRANTO were being overhauled in Liverpool, so that she will become a passenger line.

---

[23] NCO = Non-Commissioned Officer

Anyway, she was a good "Trooper".

Last night at the Cameronia we saw "The Bride goes Wild," with Van Johnson, not bad. Tonight we won't be going, so we will go to the MMG club for a massive supper.

So Alfie Peers has gone in the Army, poor beggar, he has to do five years in the Terriers when he comes out in June 1950. But if I had as long to as he had, I would be on my way home now.

If possible, could you tell me which of the following bombed areas have been built on:

Arabic   English
١   1. Top of Leasowe Road
٢   2. Colville Road
٣   3. Is the Sandy Lane – Claremont Road area finished
٤   4. School Lane
٥   5. Coliseum and Green Lane

I am enclosing three snaps which I bought from the Silver Photo Shop. number one is of the Blue Kettle Club, Ismailia. I was there last year and it is quite a decent place. Number 2 is a group of Felahins, or Mohammedhan women, and no 3 is an Arab.

So I must finish as there seems to be nothing new this week.

Much love to all,
David

P.S. Photo no 4 is of the Mosque at Port Fouad, which was just be Seaview Holiday Camp. D.
I played a bit of table tennis this morning against an experienced player, anyway I won one out of eight games. I must get a shave now (one a week), and then go to the pictures to see Bonar Colleano[24] in "Once a Jolly Swagman."
(Some extra xxx for Mum's Birthday).

---

24 Bonar Colleano died in a car crash exiting the Queensway tunnel, Birkenhead, in 1958

12th May 1949
AG1(b) Branch
GHQ
M.E.L.F.

Dear Mum and Dad,

Very many thanks for the two pairs of socks and the shirt received today. They had been on the way for over four weeks and I was beginning to get worried about them.

I am taking advantage of the fact that there are no flies around to interrupt me, you see, in the GHQ offices flies are abnormally scarce, and I am on Branch duty sergeant, or rather, senior NCO. This is my first duty sergeant since I was promoted Cpl, and I should do about three more.

In the office work is getting tougher as there are only three of us there now to manage two sections. Then on 4th June we are taking over AG9, but unless we get Vera Pearson in to help that will be the limit, and I'll tell him so, (Maj Parry). He'll have to get someone in then.

I think the general idea is that Vera will be coming to AG1(b), as she is the AG9 expert. Even in 1(b) and (c) work is pouring in, (and out).

Also, if she does come, I stand a much better chance of getting leave, at the end of June (Crikey, that's *next month*). On second thoughts July will be too late, as I will not have long enough to do. It's nice to know anyway.

Whereas I am due for demob about 14th September, she is also due to return home on 14th September, so we may go together.

There are 80 days to the time when I shall start to pack, and then I shall draw big pays, etc.

The weather has cooled off today. The Egyptian Gazette has stated that the early heat has broken, and the temperatures reached were from 75° (very low) at Port Said, to 118° at Aswan. At Fayid the temperature touched 112°. And the flies elsewhere but GHQ are terrible.

It gets dark at 7.0pm now. My duty finishes at 7.30pm, and then I will go straight to MMG, have a damn good plate of eggs and chips etc, and then get back. The senior N.C.O does 2½ hours duty every six weeks, not bad.

I finally managed to get through to 156 Transit Camp by radio last Tuesday and got the figures which three Branches were going mad for. But the Transit Camp got a good telling off.

We got a new batch of A.T.S. (WRAC) in GHQ last Monday, and everyone stares at the white legs of them. We can't believe that people are as white as that in England. There have been a lot of WRNS in as well as female civilians. I don't know what the place is coming to.

When is Harvest Sunday at church, and how is the choir getting on?

It doesn't seem a couple of months since you went to Anglesey last year, but you're almost going again. Think that when you get back I'll be packing.

I've had the photos of Caernarvon and Harlech Castle enlarged, and they are terrific. Harry says that the one of the Roman Ruins near Shrewsbury is the best photo I've got.

On Saturday the film is called "The Street with No Name," and I don't intend to miss it.

The duty clerk, (my relief), is almost here so I must pack up and make out my report.

Much love to all,
David

14th May 1949
AG1(b) Branch
GHQ
M.E.L.F.

Dear Mum and Dad,

I was emptying my pockets a moment ago and I found a letter which I should have posted last Tuesday. And yet I could have sworn I had posted it. It reminded me of that film "Easy Money" when Petula Clark pulled out the football pools form after they had found that they had found that they had won, and she found she hadn't posted the coupon.

Brad has only just been saying that really although demob seems as far away as ever, it is really very near, and for him it is too near to be comfortable as he has no money saved. He should go home about the middle of July, or when I come back off leave. My leave has now been put further back to the first two weeks of July.

Yesterday, (Saturday), was my morning off. Every clerk is entitled to one Saturday morning off each month, so it works out that there are three off from AG1 each Saturday.

In AG1 now there are:
Group
Chief clerk Sgt Collis 114
Chief clerk AG1(a) Sgt Smith Reg
Chief clerk AG1(b) and (c) Cpl Howard 118
A/Chief clerk AG1(a) Cpl Leask 110
Clerks AG1(a) L/Cpl Compton 139
Rfn Boyles Reg
Clerks AG1(b)and(e) Pte Stephenson 139
Pte O'Neill 137

Registry L/Cpl Digges 117
Pte Dipper 145
Orderly Gnr Barnes 111

It is still not warm enough to go swimming. The Egyptians say it has been the coldest and longest winter they have ever known (interrupted by a fly). For the rest of this letter I will put a cross X wherever a fly has interrupted me, they're terrible.

Even on a windy day like this there are plenty of them.

Tonight, of course, is the pictures as usual, then we go to the MMG for a heaped plate of eggs and chips. Next Sunday is May 1st, and come time in June we hope to have another Derby Day Fête.

I see New Brighton beat Wrexham 2-0, what a shock, and Taffy Davies (who comes from Wrexham), couldn't believe it.

The socks should be arriving any day now, which will give me seven good pairs of socks to start the summer. I managed to get three good woolen pairs by a bit of luck. But I will need them all.

There are now 98 days to go to the end of July, so those are the days I consider, as the rest will hardly count.

I have just got back from the Cameronia where we saw "Take My Life" with Greta Gynt and Hugh Williams. Quite good.

I hope that tomorrow will be warm enough to go into KD as dress until 2nd May is optional. On the 2nd (next Monday), we have to wear KD all the time, so that is when my BD goes away for good till I am in England again.

Well, being in bed now I will finish and post both the letters. I hope you haven't been worrying too much as it makes me worry just as much as you.

Much love to all,
David

15th May 1949
AG1(b) Branch
GHQ
M.E.L.F.

Dear Mum and Dad,

Many thanks for your letter and Pat's which I received last night at 10pm.

    I don't know what is going on out here, but I can't get brown, nor even red. Because a couple of minutes in the sun and I am scorched, of course my arms are OK as they are continually exposed.

    A lot of blokes seem to think I have only just come out here, and they're not half surprised to find that I am one of the national servicemen who have been out here longest of all. And I don't think you'll find many national servicemen who have been out here longer than me.

    There is a rumour that we will be getting demobbed at the docks when we arrive home. This seems to apply mainly to Liverpool as Southampton has Aldershot within a stones throw. But if you could check up on that!

    So Dr Barr has gone. What happens now? Anyhow I won't have any Territorial business to mess things up, as I am quite sure it would. But those poor B****s who are coming in the Army now have five years of it after they are out.

Last night at the Cameronia we saw "Street with no name," typical American gangster film. And tonight is "I See Ice," with George Formby.

I didn't think there is any need to say that the temperature is getting hotter every day, but has not gone as high as during the heat wave when it touched 112°F. It must reach 126°F by the middle-end of August. I am under the mosquito net at the moment taking refuge from the fierce onslaughts of the flies!

There are now 76 days to go before I start to get ready, and at the end of this month there will be 61 days.

Next Saturday is my Saturday off again. It seems no time since the last one.

The temperature is 116°F and still shooting upwards. I don't think that it will get much hotter now, we have just had the first of the "*Khamsins*" which are warm winds coming from the centre of the Sahara but keep the temperature steady at about 120°F.

Tonight we saw "The small back room" at the Cameronia, a story of bomb research during the war.

Well, I'll have to pack this up as I can't think of anything else to write about.

Much love to all,
David

May 1949
AG1(b) Branch
GHQ
M.E.L.F.

Dear Mum & Dad,

The news I have had to tell you hasn't amounted to much after all. My name did go on the promotions board but it never came out, probably because they had too many names. Only 20 names came out, out of about 40 that went. So, it looks as if it will have to wait until the next Official Board in three to weeks' time. Unless they hold an emergency one to get the next out, which rarelty happens. In this case I should know within a week.

The other news about demob has come out, and although it is faster than before, it is not fast enough to get out at the beginning of August.

The release dates it gives go as far as 112 group, which starts to be demobbed on the 28th June. The average rate is two groups a month or just over, more like two groups in 28 days, a group a fortnight.

I reckon by this I will be out by 13th September, but I don't see how this is going to happen as they have to get 149 group out by June 1950. At this present rate they can only get 26 groups out by June 1950, which is group 138, 11 groups behind.

I have received another parcel of papers alright, for which many thanks.

Weather news is getting better, it is turning warmer and the high wind and freak sandstorms have stopped. The temperature now is about 60°F again.

On the next page I have made a couple of impressions of some of our coins, both sides:

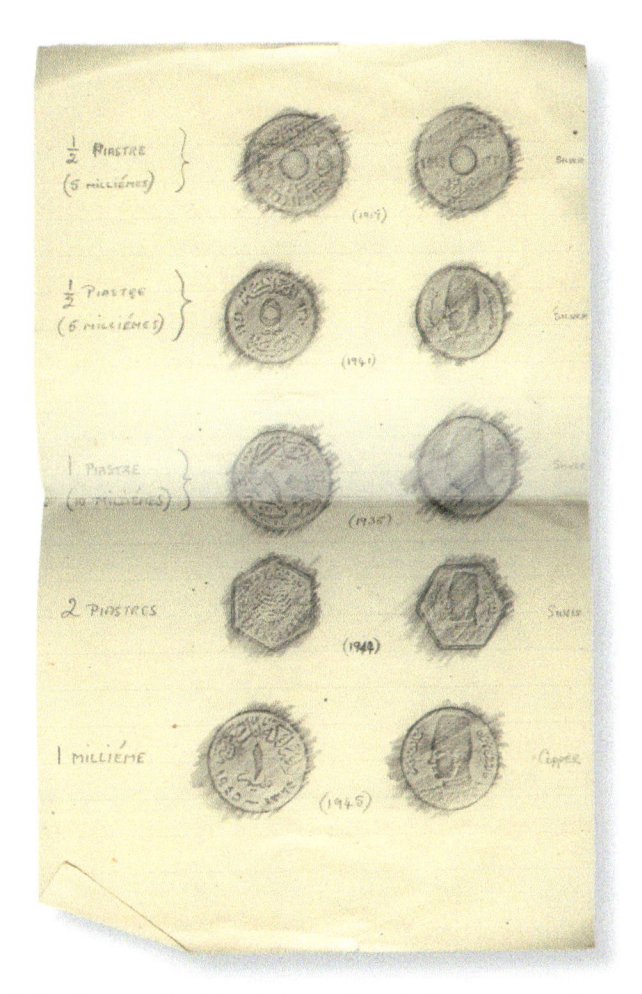

Much Binding in the Marsh is on the wireless now so I must finish as it is a sign that time is getting on.

Before I knock off, I will mention that I have four snaps left in the camera & all the rest have been taken with the extensions and portrait attachment.

Much love to all,
David xxx

22nd May 1949
AG1(b) Branch
GHQ
M.E.L.F.

Dear Mum and Dad,

From latest information received, I will be leaving here in the middle of August as group 119 is ex-MELF, 30th August 49. Till the end of July there are 70 days to go, that is the date I am counting on as "starting to pack".

Last night at the Cameronia we saw "Treasure of the Sierra Madre", a film of Mexico and plenty of Spanish, which, as before, was quite decent, and I could understand most of it.

The next time I am going in on Tuesday, to see "Out of the Blue" with George Brent, Jushan Bey, Virginia Mayo, and... *(Gap left, presumably to fill in later but didn't)*

Last Saturday was my day off, and as I am on guard today, I will be having Monday off. Not bad, eh! Then Whit Monday is in a couple of weeks and is a bank holiday. I haven't heard anything about the Derby Day Fete yet.

There are one or two starting points about the temperature here. At Ordnance Branch, GHQ, the temperature in the shade, and under a fan was 106°F. At Education Branch, GHQ, the temperature at 6am under a fan which was full on, was 80°F. The highest temperature in the normal shade up to now has been 116°F.

Yesterday 110 group went on demob and as I was on leave I helped Pat Leask across to Camp Branch with his kit bag, while he carried a case and big pack full of stuff. I imagined that it was me with my own kit bag going on demob.

Soon it will be time for me to put in for my leave. I will be taking it at either the end of June or beginning of July and I will be going to Port Fouad again.

With effect from next Monday the GHQ office hours will change, viz:

Mon, Wed, Fri: 07.30-12.30 and 2.30pm-4.30pm.
Tues, Thurs: 07.30 till 12.30.
Sat: 07.30 till 12.00.

Then in the middle of June they will change again to:

Mon-Fri: 07.30-2pm.
Sat: 07.30-1pm.

At the end of June there will be a vote for which hours are best. The present one, those of the first half of June, or O2E hours, (the last half of June).

We will revert to the present hours at the end of June.

Also in June, the staff of AG3 and AG4 (officers records), will move to O2E (OR's Records) so that all the records will be together, with the exception of M.S. Branch which deal with the records of the Staff Officers of GHQ

AG1(b) takes over AG9 on 4th June.

What is the latest news from St Hilarys? Has anyone else come in the Forces? And when are you getting the telephone? Halsall's is 7464 isn't it? What is the approximate course of Green Leas Road?

Well, I think that is all for now.

Much love to all,
David

27th May 1949
AG1(b) Branch
GHQ
M.E.L.F.

Dear Mum and Dad,

It is warming up considering out here and I have ten more hours to do in Battledress. Ten more hours and the next time I shall wear it will be on the train Home.

From more information received Gp 118 is leaving Ceylon at the end of July. Ceylon is a fortnights sailing time from Port Said.

The flies are getting terrible as it gets hotter. It is now hotter than a hot English Summers Day. Phew!!

Pat Leask is going on demob in about a fortnights time. Then comes Tony Collis, Johnny Digges, and me.

There are five more hours in BD left now.

I have just come back from the pictures where we saw "Things Happen at Night" with Robertson Hare, Gordon Harker, and Jerry Marsh.

1st May 1949

Yesterday there was a fire at work and we had it out before the fire brigade arrived. It was only an old shed so we think it was a practice. One bloke saw the fire first, looked at it and turned away with his hands in his pockets.

I have now finished with BD until I get home. The weather has warmed up a dickens of a lot in the last few days. It is now touching 90°F. But it has still to go to 126°F.

There are now 91 days to the time when I shall have to start to hand over at work and start packing.

When I left for Liverpool I had 578 days to do till the same date, now 91.

A week tomorrow (Monday), Maj Parry comes back, and I think Mary is coming to say goodbye next week sometime

| | |
Flies Flies Flies

You will notice how the last three words are written, the cause is the flies. I got so mad in the end I shouted "Gerrout!"

Many thanks for Dad's letter received yesterday. I will be looking forward to getting the snaps as everything is so dim.

Then I see Keith is playing for Wallasey in the Youth Leagues. I can imagine him as a sort of discovery, his head was big enough at one time but what's it like now. It was just above normal size last December. What does he think of Wolves winning the cup.

In Cairo, the police have found three big secret ammo dumps, which they think were going to be used for terrorist activities. The biggest in 22 Docki Street, Shubra, Cairo, contained 400 hand grenades, 1000 sticks of gelignite, eight machine guns, four Vickers Guns, two sten guns, 13 Tommy guns, eight fruit baskets filled with sticks of explosives and cordite, molotov bombs, large quantitys of gunpowder, millions of cartridges, and a workshop. But Cairo had been saved.

Jenny Banton has signed on in the WRAC (ATS), and the signing on ceremony was the first of its kind in the Middle East. there is an account of it in the Egyptian Gazette, and as she is the senior of the six who signed on, her name was just in the paper.

I have seen a weather forecast in the Egyptian Gazette for the first time. It says:

"Forecast for next 24 hours commencing noon on April 30th to noon May 1st. Lower Egypt and Cairo: Northerly winds changing and becoming southerly on the coast tomorrow. Clean or some high and medium clouds later. Weather remaining pleasant but temperature rising slightly tomorrow."

And that seems to be all for now, so…

Much love to all,
David

29th May 1949
AG1(b) Branch
GHQ
M.E.L.F.

Dear Mum & Dad,

If you get this letter on Thursday, there will be 59 days to go to the time when I have to start packing up. That is just over eight weeks.

111 Group is leaving on Tuesday and 114 Group is leaving on 12th July.

Whereas before I have been asking about blokes who have come into the Army since I came in, now it is the other way round. Do you know of anyone who has been demobbed lately? I suppose Len Robinson and Len Davies are well out by now. I myself expect to be demobbed on the 15th September, as most of the groups going home now arrive almost when the group opens. 118 opens on the 9th September, so it is possible for me to be home on the 9th (or the early hours of the 10th).

The weather is still keeping steady with a fairly low temperature of 104°F in the shade.

Many thanks for Dad's and Pat's letter received a couple of days ago. I got the cutting about the Moascar Garrison Church choir. Moascar is about 25 miles away and is part of Ismailia, it is also the Headquarters of the British Troops in Egypt and Mediterranean Command and also the Headquarters of the R.A.F in the Middle East. Of course, both these HQ's come under G.H.Q., M.E.L.F.

You say you are going on a week's holiday to Anglesey again, but Dad says that he has another week due to him, when is he taking that?

Tomorrow, we start new working hours, starting at 7.30am. We have to get up at 5am.

But now here is the news, *My Relief Has Come.*

Actually, he will be here for a week and then he goes on three weeks leave till the 4th July. Then after he comes back, I will be handing over to hm & teaching him the job for a week, and then I go on a fortnight's leave till the last week in July.

When I come back, I will still be teaching him the job and I will chief adviser in the office and taking it easy. This period after I come back off leave will last for three weeks, and then, *I Pack Up* and go home.

So that's that.

There is a dance on in the Sergeant's Mess at the moment and the band is quite decent. We are only 20 yards from it.

Tonight, at the Cameronia is "Spring in Park Lane" with Anna Neagle and Michael Wilding. I have seen it once while I have been here but I am going to see it again.

Last night we saw "Portrait from Life" which was very good.

We do get Whit Monday off and also the King's Birthday (9th June) is a holiday out here. But on the 19th is a parade in the morning.

Up to now there has been four bokes of 111 group in this tent yapping about demob, what they have done, and the trains they will be getting from Aldershot & London. There are only two people I know really well in this group. They are Bob Leach of Maryport, Cumberland, and Pete Grant of Grimsby, Lincolnshire.

It is almost time for me to be going to the pictures. The dog has been fed (we're looking after him for a while, while Jock's away) and so we can move off.

Much love to all,
David xxx

6th June 1949
AG1(b) Branch
GHQ
M.E.L.F.

Dear Mum and Dad,

Very many thanks for Mum's letter which I received on Saturday night, and also the letter from Magada which was enclosed.

If you get this letter on Friday, there will be then 51 days to go, that is seven weeks and seven letters. Actually on Friday there will exactly 100 days to go to the time when I will definitely be home.

So I see you will have to be getting another dog. If you were to come out here, you would see the real dogs. Dogs that are here primarily to scare the wogs away, and attack if necessary. The main type is the mixed breed of Alsatian and Collie. The only dogs I have seen in England that are better than ours out here, are the Welsh sheepdogs. And I think that is only for intelligence which is only slightly higher.

The latest rumour is that all personnel with less than three months to do, will not be able to get leave. Now I will have only one month to do when I go on leave at the end of this month.

About the allotment, there is not enough active service period left for me to do, so I can't increase it. Instead I have had to put my pay up to £2 a week. But it is nice to know that there are things which I can't do as I haven't got long enough to serve.

The other day the Supervisory Warrant Officer of A.G. Branch came in to the office, and said "We will be losing you soon, won't we, Corpl Howard?" I think that is why he brought my relief in, although I still think it is a couple of weeks early.

Whit went down OK, and the weather was cooler than of late. Yesterday and today have been very cool, and it has been cold at night. Yesterday itself is probably what one might call 'the perfect English Summer's day.'

Yesterday, there was a big fire at the Camp QM (stores). Everything in the shed was destroyed, from wirelesses to mosquito nets. The whole camp dashed over, mainly, I think, to watch it, and not to put it out.

Well, there doesn't seem to be much else to write about. Don't forget to give Keith a shake about that letter of his.

Much love to all,
David

P.S. Am sending a letter to Magada with this one.
The address is
Señorita Magada Whort,
SAN LORENZO 227,
PERGAMINO,
Provincia De Buenos Aires,
República ARGENTINA.

Just received a letter from Mary Hodge in Cornwall. Will tell you about it in next letter on Sunday.

17th June 1949
AG1(b) Branch
GHQ
M.E.L.F.

Dear Mum and Dad,

Very many thanks for four parcels of papers, a letter from Dad, a letter from Keith. I have also had a letter from Mary Hodge, and one from Phyllis Evans. I think they all came in a rush, practically one a day.

Before I go any further, I want to correct a little sentence of Dad's. He said that he thinks I will be packing in eight weeks time. Well, you're wrong, I will be almost at Liverpool or Southampton in that time.

Eightweeks today is the middle of August, and groups are leaving here a month before their demob dates. 113 group is the next to go, and they go on 22nd June. Then 114 group leave on 11th July.

I have put in my pass and it has been approved and signed by the Branch. The next is Camp, who are not keen on giving passes to persons with less than three months to do, and especially to those with less than two months to do, like me, when I go on leave.

I am trying to go to Seaview from 13.15 hrs Tuesday 5th July, till 08.00 hrs 20th July.

This morning Johnny O'Neill showed me a photo of his Platoon at the RASC Training Depot, Kiskee McMunn Barracks, Colchester.

On looking through all the chaps (20 of them), I stopped at one who was second from the right in the middle row. Then I recognised him, no other than Billy Window Jnr. I checked and

Johnny said his name was Windsor and that now that he came to think of it, he did come from Wallasey. His group is 137, due out in March, 1950.

In the office, a new Major is coming to take over Maj Parry's place on 17th July. Maj Parry goes home at the beginning of August.

The weather is staying very steady, not too hot, and not cold at night. Here is a cool breeze. The general impression is that from now on the weather will go no hotter except for an occasional day or two. At the moment it is steady at 105°F.

flies   flies

Last Sunday we went across the Bitter Lake to the Blue Lagoon. It is a lake in itself joined to the Bitter Lake by a narrow bottleneck. It is in the Sinai Desert which extends into Arabia. We had two RASC Launches to take us across, (by the way, it was an AG Branch outing), from the Fanana Wharf.

Fanana Wharf is a quayside and small dock for the smaller ships in the Suez Canal.

On the way across we passed seven cargo and passenger lines, but not one was British. One was Spanish, one Swedish, and the others unknown. We led a very strong pair of field glasses, Army type. I will draw a map with this letter.

Leaving at 11.0am, we got back at 5pm.

Sunday
The picture at the Cameronia last night was "Call Northside 777" with James Stewart. He's the chap who always seems to be dead cheesed and *alakeefik*, a tired looking article.

Tomorrow I am putting my pass into the Company Office. And this is where the difficulty begins, as it is more than likely that they will turn it down on the grounds that I have only two months to do here, and only a couple of weeks when I come off leave. But if this is the case, Maj Parry will write out a case and get it signed by either Lt Col Tucker or Brigadier Bradshaw, the DAG. at one time the DAG used to be a Maj General.

HMS Vanguard is on a visit to Port Said at the moment, and some of the sailors are down here at GHQ, they are all over the canal zone for reasons of sport. The crew of a battleship is enough to have organised teams for all sorts of games, as well as a boxing tournament at the Kitchener Road Stadium, Moascar (HQ BTE, ISMAILIA).

If you get this letter on Thursday there will be 38 days to go. Brad and Harry (114 group) are going in a fortnight or just over according to shipping.

Much love to all,
David

Overleaf: map of the Bitter Lake and Sinai Desert

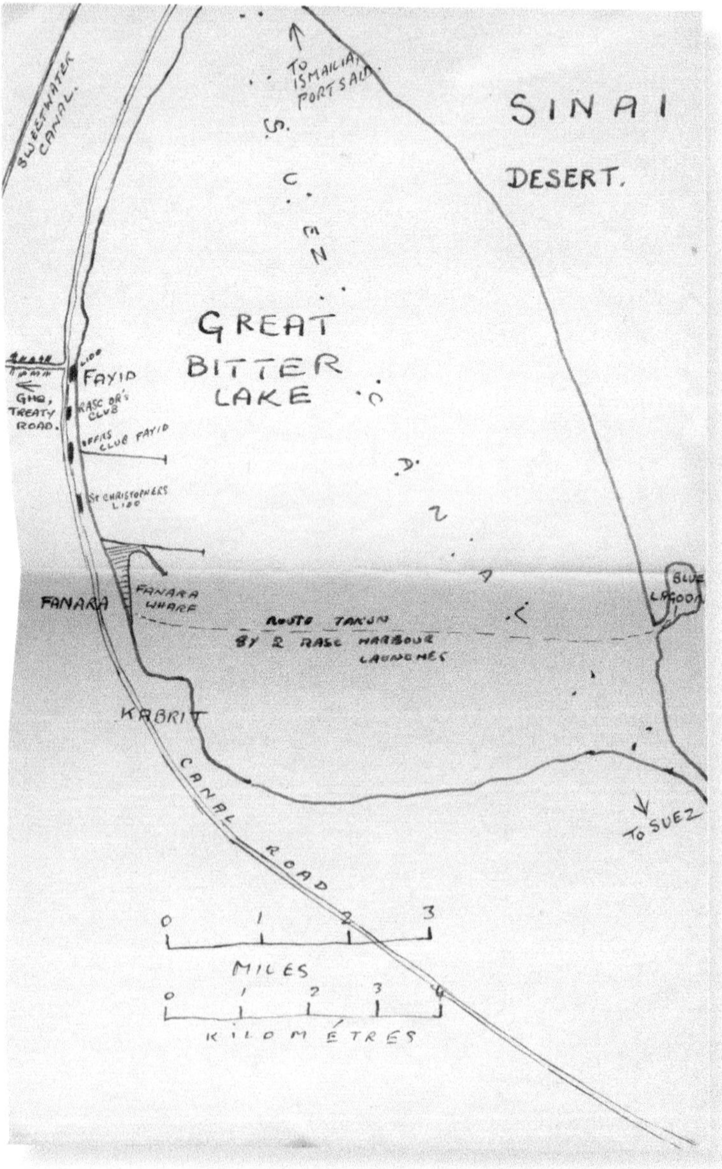

SWEETWATER CANAL.
TO ISMAILIA PORT SAID
SINAI
DESERT.
GREAT BITTER LAKE
LIDO
FAYID
GHQ, TREATY ROAD.
RASC OR'S CLUB
OFFRS CLUB FAYID
St CHRISTOPHERS LIDO
FANARA
FANARA WHARF
BLUE LAGOON
ROUTE TAKEN BY 2 RASC HARBOUR LAUNCHES
KABRIT
CANAL ROAD
TO SUEZ
0 1 2 3
MILES
0 1 2 3 4
KILOMÉTRES

June 1949
AG1(b) Branch
GHQ
M.E.L.F.

Dear Mum & Dad,

I hope you receive Magada's letter at the same time as this. I will repeat the address:
Magada Whort,
San Lorenzo 227
Pergamino
Provincia de Beunos Aires
Republica ARGENTINA

Then the usual.

Well up to now, the weather has been much better than has ever been hope for. In comparison with last year, it is cooler (although in the 100's), there are more breezes and it has been refreshingly cool at night. Last year the temperature was abhorable and flies came in their millions. Flies this year are only a d**** nuisance.

I have been swimming again, or rather, getting a hot bath.

Hi Majesty's Battleship "LIVERPOOL" arrived at the C-in-C's peers this morning and trips in four admirals' launches, starting tomorrow, are free. The "LIVERPOOL" will be followed by a cruiser in a couple of weeks' time. It has caused quite a sensation.

It seems pretty certain now that we will be going Seaview Holiday Camp the first week in August. So, here's to good food and good waiters.

Keith's School Certificate Paper in French seemed easy so I am quite sure he has got at least a credit in that. As for the others, I can't tell, but by the sounds of it, he seems to have passed easily enough.

Is there any more news about the choir and their activities, and who is still in it?

Don't forget that any papers or magazines, books etc are always very welcome.

Well, Mum, although I have forgotten what your cooking at home is like, my stomach still tells me I am hungry.

Much love to all
David xxx

24th June 1949
AG1(b) Branch
GHQ
M.E.L.F.

Dear Mum and Dad,

Very many thanks for two letters received together, one from Pat was also included as well as the snaps.

Keith looks as if he has just been picked to play for England, and Pat, erll, it's quite good. By the way, give Pat my congrats on the snap she took of Mum, it really was very good. It is an angle which I have never looked at before. But that snap of the choir is the best of the lot.

Still, they are all very good, and many thanks.

Today I got my big pay through, which means I now have £13.10.0 ready cash. Also I sent a letter to Seaview booking for 5th – 20th July inclusive, and today a new order came out that personnel can now take entitled leave during their last three months of service. So it is almost certain that I shall be going. All I have to wait for now is a letter from Seaview confirming reservation.

Brad, Harry and Tony Collis are going home on demob in just over a week's time. They are the next N.S. group to leave here, (114). Five weeks on Sunday I pack my kit, actually 4½ weeks from when you get this letter.

There was a big trooper in the Bitter Lake today, passing through between Suez and Port Said. The "Empire Halladale" is due up next Sunday.

Soon the mid-August shipping programme will arrive, and by the end of July, I should be able to tell on what ship I will be sailing, and also to what port. I want to go to Southampton, but

90% of troopships go to Liverpool, as it is now the second largest port (next to London).

As for demob leave, the minimum is 24 days.

I am sending a photograph of a "Mummy" with this letter. It is the real thing and is in the antique shop "Khan Kalil" in the shopping centre, I have been right up to it and had a good look, and could see the way everything had been preserved.

When the box is closed there is the carving on the front.

I am not going to the pictures tonight, (Sunday) as it is "London Belongs to Me" which I have seen before.

Much love to all,
David

The temperature here is keeping down terrifically, and there has been a continual light breeze for a week now which has been quite cool. Steve has not been promoted to L/Cpl on my recommendation. He has been in AG1(b) for almost seven months, I was in for almost eight months before I was promoted. You are going to Anglesey on 23rd July so I will write from Port Said and address the letters or cards to:

Mr Williams,
Garnedd Fawr,
Gaerwen,
Anglesey,
N. Wales.
U.K.

But send my letters to AG1(b).

6th July 1949
AG1(b) Branch
GHQ
M.E.L.F.

Dear Mum and Dad,

I arrived here at 1.30pm after a good journey.

Going through the events of the day, I got up at 5.45am and after coming back from breakfast we packed my kit and handed everything into the Coy stores. I left camp at 8.45am and caught the 9.15am Canal South District Welfare bus from the Fayid Shopping Centre to French Square, ISMAILIA.

I then had an hour to wait for a train so I went into the Station NAAFI, had a short snack and got a Second Class return ticket to Port Said.

The train left at 11am and arrived at Port Said main station at 12.40pm. There was a truck waiting, and that got me through Port Said to the Port Fouad ferry. There I went across on the Ferry and walked to Seaview.

It is just the same as when I was there this time last year.

After booking in I got to the tent and relaxed. The weather has not been hot, but I was covered in sand and sweat after the 100 mile journey, so after having a shower I got into some clean civvies and went for a snack which is called tea. The tea was terrific, and there was sugar on the table.

The next meal I will be able to have is dinner at 6.30pm. The time now is 5pm.

It's a terrific change after Camp. You are waited on hand and foot, you are absolutely free, no walking the mile to GHQ & back four times a day. In other words, everything is at hand, and all you do is relax. How people stay in camp for leave I don't know.

I go back to work as usual on 20th July and I should be out of Egypt three to four weeks after that.

I said goodbye to Harry and Brad when I left camp as I won't see them again. They should be going very soon, (a week or so).

At Port Said today, I saw the old troopship "LANCASHIRE," registered and bound for Liverpool. It was packed with troops and is a regular troopship on the Liverpool – MELF – FARELF run. FARELF is the abbreviation for Far East Land Forces.

I left work clear, that is, I left nothing for anyone to clear up. Up to then we had had plenty of work, which at times necessitated to get clear in time.

S/Sgt Mills came back from Cyprus on Monday and so everything is in his hands which will enable us to see if he can manage it without my assistance. When I get back there will be a new officer there. He will be Maj Brett, and is taking over Maj Parry's job when he goes on Python in August.

The weather is keeping cool, down in the 90°s, and there is a continual cool breeze. The weather this summer has been nowhere near hot, just like a hot, fine English Summers day continually.

There is a dance on at the moment on the floor, it is a rhumba and will be followed by a samba.

I want this letter to catch the Seaview morning post, so I will write again the day after tomorrow.

Much love to all,
David

13th July 1949
AG1(b) Branch
GHQ
M.E.L.F.

Dear Mum and Dad,

I have been at Seaview for seven days and it has been just the job.

On Saturday night we went into Port Said and passing along the Boulevard Fouad 1er we saw cabaret just starting so we went in to see what it was like. There was a cover charge at 10½ f.

Inside it was the usual night club style and at 11-0-clock a floor show started. There were six girls dancing separately to Eastern music. You know the style, with the dancers wearing all sorts of trinkets, but not very many clothes, most of what they wore was transparent. At 12 midnight the dancing started, and carried on till 1am when we all bailed out. I got to bed at 2am.

Then on Sunday morning we went to Port Fouad Park, which has quite a few tropical trees and date palms. Of course there is grass everywhere, and there is a main avenue. At 11am a group of French convent children came in accompanied by two French nuns who seemed very friendly. Everyone spoke French. They were on a sort of picnic while the sun was still cool (80°F). French sounds a lot better when spoken as it was then.

As you probably know already, Port Fouad is a French Colonial Town mainly, and all the houses are in massive grounds.

The weather gets very hot here in the morning, yet Alexandria's hottest for the last few days has only been 98° (Egyptian Mail).

I have been into town quite a few times and the troopships I have seen while crossing on the ferry, (it passes within 50 yards of the berthing stage), have seen the troopers 'LANCASHIRE', 'ORBITA,' and 'EMPRESS OF AUSTRALIA,' all registered at Liverpool, bound for Liverpool, and full of troops. 113 and some of 114 group left in the EMPRESS OF AUSTRALIA early this morning. The rest of 114 groups are leaving on the EMPIRE PRIDE next Wednesday 20th, some of 115 will probably go on this ship as well.

When I go back to work next Wednesday, I should be leaving Egypt about four weeks from then.

I forgot to add to my account of the Cabaret that there were some American sailors there who were from the American tanker 'FRIEDRICKSBURG', which has developed engine trouble at one of the ten main Port Said berths.

We have been playing snooker a lot lately, and, as partners, two of us have won two out of three proper games.

The night before last we saw the picture "For them that trespass" at the Seaview RAF cinema, and last night we went to the 'El Dorado' in Port Said to see 'The Three Musketeers' with Don Ameche and the Ritz Brothers. On this programme there was a French film, the trailer to an Egyptian film, and a French newsreel. Then the big picture was in English of course.

The meals here are smashing, and the tea is on the table in a pot.

A présent je lis un livre qui s'appelle "L'Homme Invisible" par H.G. Wells, je suis sûr de quoi tu as entendu parler du livre. C'est un roman d'un homme qui s'est tourné vers la science et lui a demandé si l'homme poussait enfin réaliser ce vieux rêve qui lui demeurait la toute-puissance. J'espère que Keith le peuve traduire.

If we do anything interesting tonight, I will sling it in with this letter. But now I must finish for tea. I will write again on Sunday and post it on the Monday as I think you are going to Anglesey a week on Saturday.

Much love to all,
David

P.S. Will be sending one or two photos tomorrow, separate to this letter. They are postcard size. Played table tennis tonight and won three out of four sets.

1st August 1949
AG1(b) Branch
GHQ
M.E.L.F.

Dear Mum and Dad,

IF I'M LUCKY I'LL BE HOME THIS MONTH. The following are the possible moves:

Move into transit a week on Friday (12.8.49), and sail on 16th August.

Move into transit two weeks on Thursday and sail on the "ARUNDEL CASTLE" for Southampton.

So, when you get this letter it will be no use sending any more papers, or anything by seamail. Actually, I think there will be some papers on the way now that I will not receive, having gone on demob.

At work there are being big change rounds and office movements. Alex Mills has finished work and goes into transit tomorrow, Tuesday.

The latest unofficial news is that 117 group is next Monday 8th August.

From the time I leave Port Said to the time I arrive at Lime Street will be at the most about 14 days.

Have you any suggestions as to what to do when I get home? I would like to have a week in Wallasey and a week in Wales. Then get to work. If Dad thinks I should allow more time to get my job when let him say so, I won't mind. As far as I know I will be getting 28 days leave.

I am still aware of the fact that the schools have finished and that there will be quite a lot of jobs taken. On the other hand, I have finished my compulsory army service, and as far as I know firms will not take on chaps who still have it to do. 95% of those leaving secondary schools will have to go in the Forces.

All the schools will have broken up and all S.C. and H.S.C. exams over. Before they go back I'll be half way through my demob leave

From now on it looks as if I will be sending letters in the form of bulletins. It looks pretty definite about sailing on the 22nd, so I should now be writing my last half dozen letters. Actually you should get four at the most after this, and that is writing

*letter ends here - page missing**

24th July 1949
AG1(b) Branch
GHQ
M.E.L.F.

Dear Mum and Dad,

When I got back to camp last Monday evening I found two letters and three packages of papers waiting. The snaps were, as you say, very good, and have brightened up the collection quite a bit. But soon I will be sending home parcels of various odds and ends which I will not want to carry Home.

Going back again to Monday, here is a summary of the journey back. I got up at 7.30am, which was rather early, but the others had had to get up at 7am as they had to catch an earlier train than me. You can't really sleep when there is a lot of bustling going on around.

I hung around until midday and then got a coach from the camp, across the Ferry to Port Said Station. Now, on the other side of the Ferry, we were stopped (15 of us) by Customs Officials who searched the kit of two of us (not me).

We got to the station OK and the train pulled out for Ismailia dead on time (1.15pm). We arrived at Ismailia at 2.25pm which is pretty good going. From there I walked into the town and to French Square. I caught a Canal South District Welfare Bus to Fayid, arriving at 4pm, which means that I probably broke the record for the journey, only 2 ¾ hours from Port Said to Fayid, (90 miles).

I was settled in for the last few weeks at 7.30pm.

At work things started to move. Yesterday there was nothing to do as everything had been cleaned except a bit of typing, but at 10.30am yesterday just after I had got everything clear I had to go on duty clerk. So I bet there will be another stack of work on Monday to clear.

Alex Mills is going Home next Sunday and will be sailing on the "DILWASA" which is leaving Port Said for Liverpool on 5th August. 116 groups have not left Canal South yet, but from Canal North District, 116 group sailed for Liverpool last Friday. I expect that our 116 group will either go into transit or sail next Friday 29th July.

In 2 Coy GHQ, 117 group are being documented for release tomorrow, Monday. The end of next week should see me on group number 2.

I expect to sail on either the
RMS ARUNDEL CASTLE
ETD (estimated time of departure): 22nd Aug, Port Said.
ETA (estimated time of arrival:) 1st Sep, Southampton.
Or
MV GEORGIC
ETD: 6th Sep, Port Said
ETA: 14th Sep, Liverpool

But I don't think it will be as late as the GEORGIC.

If I go on the ARUNDEL CASTLE, I will go into transit about 18th Aug, and finish work on 15th August.

A week tomorrow is 1st August. So the conclusion is that I haven't long to go now.

I have just got back from the Cameronia where I saw "The Guinea Pig" with Richard Attenborough.

Have you got a phone in yet? If you don't think that you will be getting one in before September, you had better give me Halsall's number, which I think is Wallasey 7464.

The time is now ten minutes past nine so I must finish this letter for now.

Much love to all,
David

26th July 1949
AG1(b) Branch
GHQ
M.E.L.F.

Dear Mum & Dad,

Very many thanks for two letters and one form Keith, received on Friday. I have remembered the telephone number, which is Mrs Scott, Wallasey 8901.

I am glad to hear you enjoyed yet another holiday in Anglesey and also that there is another week to come when I get home. What do you think would be the best idea or suggestion?

How is the weather now? Could you get hold of the normal temperature in England at the moment? Here it is 100°F and quite cool, of course, the sun is still shining and has been for four months approx.

For the second time in two weeks, I have been told by Frenchmen how well I speak and read French. They both said that out of a thousand Englishmen who I speak French I would be the best. So that sound alright.

As to Spanish, I have only met two people and they were Italians. But they were rather astonished, as an "Englishman speaking Spanish" is rather incredible.

When is the harvest Sunday at St Hilary's, and ask Keith to let me know the latest news from church? By the way he will have to reply to this letter straight away almost as it is possible to move into xxx [can't read] next Tuesday, but not likely.

Four Sundays from now I hope to be walking/strolling along the prom or something similar.

Get a bath

Go to the cinema (not one built of mud & iron chains)

Travel in buses (not cattle cars)
See some rain and cool off in general
Walk around without being pestered

Live in houses with all their conveniences and not in tents (100 yards to the nearest lavatory, 30 yards to get a drink or wash, and the water is never cold).

And worst of all is the fact that there is sand everywhere.

In the office the movements have been completed, and Steve is now virtually the chief clerk. WE have seen about his "second".

Up to now Alex Wills (S/Sgt) has been amusing himself by reading all day. He is 120 Group but will be going on a Class B release with 117 Group which sails from Port Said on the 16th (next Tuesday).

So, at the moment the office is as follows

Group
Reg	Chief Clerk	AGI	WOI WADE
139	Chief Clerk	AGI (b&C)	L/Cpl STEPHENSON
137	A/C/Clerk	AGI (c)	Pte O'NEILL
137	Clerk	AGI (b)	Pte TAYLOR
135	Typist		Pte HILLIER
REG	Chief Clerk	AGI (a & MP)	Sgt SMITH
121	A/C/ Clerk	AGI (MP)	L/Cpl RYAN
249	Clerk	AGI (a)	Pte ?
145	Clerk	AGI (MP)	Pte DIPPER

So that S/Sgt Mills and myself are spare at the moment waiting for shipping. Still, we go up to work to show there's no ill feeling.

And that seems to be the xxx [can't read] for now.

Much love to all,

David xxx

14th August 1949
AG1(b) Branch
GHQ
M.E.L.F.

Dear Mum and Dad,

Many thanks for Dad's letter received yesterday, Saturday. I have noted the telephone number which, from memory, is Mrs Scott, Wallasey 8901, and don't worry about what you can get and what you can't get, all I want is a bath, a fire, and something to eat; oh, and a bed as well!

It is pretty certain now that we won't be moving off before 4th September. You see, 117 group went on demob yesterday, and they will be filling up the two available boats next week. I don't know what is happening about the Arundel Castle, and even though she is empty I don't think she'll be taking any release personnel, in any case, we should have been informed by now if we were going to sail on it.

So the next boat is the ORDUNA, which sails from Port Said on 4th September, and then there is the GEORGIC, which sails from Port Said on 6th September. These are the only two ships that can get us home in time for demob. The GEORGIC arrives in Liverpool on 14th September, and the ORDUNA also goes to Liverpool. So I have 2½ weeks to go in GHQ.

The question now is, how to pass the time away. At the moment it is dragging terribly, as they say it always does during the last couple of weeks. I have plenty to do with regard to packing and sorting out of kit, but that only takes up a very small portion of the time.

Reading French magazines is helpful, and I was surprised at how quickly they could be read. I have one or two more photos of the area to take yet, especially in GHQ itself.

Today, I went down to the Sergeant's Mess and fetched Taffy Smith. While we were walking along the banks of the Canal, (Sweetwater), we saw four fishermen and one was holding, or rather, trying to hold up, a fish which measured four feet in length. I got a photo of it, but I don't know what it will be like.

I was very hot in the sun today, probably about 120°F, but only about 90°F in the shade. But at nights now we usually get a nice cool breeze, as at the moment (7.25pm and pitch black outside).

What time does it get dark these days in England? Our variation is about two hours per year, on 21st December, it is dark at 5.30pm, and 21st July, it is dark at 7.30pm.

In the office I have decided to take over Chief Clerk for a week and shake things up a bit. As we won't be leaving this week I may as well do something to make the next couple of weeks pass.

Yesterday I told Johnny O'Neill to check a letter that had just been typed. During that time I went over to Comd Secretariat, and on coming back a quarter of an hour later, I found that he had checked it and despatched it, and it hadn't been signed. One or two people have said that that chap is dead from the neck upwards. It strikes me he just couldn't care less. And I'm afraid that he won't get any promotion if he carries on as he is.

Taffy Smith, (Staff Sergeant), told me that he saw the chief clerk of AG Branch, (WOI[25] Tobin), and said that he didn't know what was going to happen to AG1(b) & (c) when I go on demob. The only bloke that knows anything about it is Steve, and he is the only one that office worth promoting.

I have heard that I was recommended for the full establishment (S/Sgt), but that Major Parry, being an old skinflint, wasn't having any. He even used Army envelopes to send his private mail in. I think he believes in getting as much as possible out of a person, for as little as possible.

---

25 WOI = Warrant Officer Class One

Does Dad ever see any of the ships I have mentioned in Liverpool? It looks pretty definite about docking in Liverpool now, but we will immediately go by train from Liverpool Riverside Station to London (Euston), and then from Waterloo to Aldershot. At that rate goodness knows what time of the day I should arrive.

Don't forget, it isn't much use sending papers now as they will never reach me. Another thing is, I may be sending some postal orders home by post as the amount of currency you are allowed to take into England is restricted. But if I send some orders by registered post I would like you to keep them for me as they will go towards my demob leave.

Will write again as soon as there is any more news.

Much love to all,
David

PS. I managed to write this letter on a table tonight. D

20th August 1949
AG1(b) Branch
GHQ
M.E.L.F.

Dear Mum and Dad,

I managed to get hold of a box of liquorice allsorts this afternoon and while I am writing this letter I am in the process of having a good chew. They are the first of that kind of sweet I have tasted since December 47.

Notice the change in the address. GHQ is now in M.E.L.F Postal District 17 for convenience to the Army Postal Services. One or two of these Middle East Commands have always had a postal District number. For instance, Benghazi in Cyrenaica is M.E.L.F. 6.

I am enclosing one or two cuttings from a recent issue of "Picture Post". They are rather interesting and quite true. Also I should be enclosing one or two new photos, (if I don't forget). They were taken at Port Fouad.

Last Wednesday we had our release documentation, that is, filling in our release books. In one place I had to put "address to which final payment is to be made", of course I put 68 Prospect Vale. In the release book is the railways warrant (British Railways, Third Class), the clothing coupons, which we don't get now, and Civilian Identity Card, as well as all particulars. It consisted mainly of filling in name and Home address.

After we had filled in the book we went round to the Company Stores and got a list of all kit to hand in before we go. This kit is known as "kit surplus to release scale."

Then on Friday we went for our release medical. As far as I know I am still AI, at least he says "fit for further service" and made no change in the measurement of my Pulheems[26]. We will have to have the vaccinations which I should think will be next week (Monday being the first day of the week).

We won't be moving now before the beginning of September. The ships are as follows:
(OXFORDSHIRE)
2nd Maybe an emergency ship to take 118
4th ORDUNA for Liverpool
6th GEORGIC for Liverpool

If we are going to be late for release (after 19th September). War Office are going to send another ship out which is standing by at the moment.

Is it very cold in England during September? It is still hot out here but cooling off very slightly.

I think British football started today, didn't it. I know Scotland started last week.

Taffy told me that my testimonial has gone in to the officers, and that it is marked "URGENT". It starts off; "The above named NCO of your Branch is shortly due for release, etc, etc,"

By the way, I don't like to speak too soon, but I might… I might have to change the address again yet before I go, in the first line I mean. At the same time Steve is being promoted to full corporal to carry the job on his shoulders then.

It doesn't look as if this letter will be quite as long as the last one. But I will write as soon as any news comes in, which should be before next weekend.

Much love to all,
David

---

26 Pulheems = A system of grading physical and mental fitness to serve in the British armed forces

2nd September 1949
AG1(b) Branch
GHQ
M.E.L.F.

Dear Mum and Dad,

Last night the draft rolls for personnel embarking on the S.S. OXFORDSHIRE went up on the Mess Notice Board.

I am the Assistant Draft Conducting NCO of Draft Roll 9 and proceeds on board the ship on Sunday morning. We will be going to Liverpool, but as I don't know the approximate time of arrival you will just have to keep a watch.

We arrived at 156 Transit Camp last Monday at 12.30pm after leaving Fayid at 6.30am.

I said Goodbye to everyone in rather a rush as everything has been rather a rush since we received the signal last Friday Morning.

It was rather unexpected.

In this tent are two Intelligence Corps Sergeants 118 Group who actually knew Monty (Brian Montgomery) when they were at Aldershot.

Tomorrow the Assistant Draft Conducting NCOs have to report to "A" Camp Office at 9.15am, then at 10am in the FFI Medical Inspection. At 11am we hand in currency for exchange into Sterling.

Then at 8am on Sunday morning S/Sgt Davies and myself, Sgt Howard will find ourselves in charge (or in Command) of 50 men (quite a large Draft).

We have been over to Port Said a couple of times since we arrived here and saw three good films. One at the Brittania Club, and the other two at the Rio in the Boulevard Fouad 1er.

And so as this, my last letter, comes to a close until you see the OXFORDSHIRE in England I will say Goodbye for now, and end as always,

Much love to all,
David

Fin

List of films with leading stars:

Spellbound (1945) – Ingrid Bergman & Gregory Peck
I'll Be Yours (1947) – Deanna Durbin & Tom Drake
The Spanish Main (1945) – Paul Henreid & Maureen O'Hara
Carnival (1946) – Sally Gray & Michael Wilding
Holiday Camp (1948) – Flora Robson & Jack Warner,
So Well Remembered (1947) – John Mills & Martha Scott
A Likely Story (1947) – Bill Williams & Barbara Hale
Song of Freedom (1936) – Paul Robeson
Blockheads (1938) – Lauren & Hardy
Badmen of the Border (1945) – Kirby Grant
House of Frankenstein (1944) – Boris Karloff
Les Miserables (1935) – Fredric March & Charles Laughton
The Prisoner of Shark Island (1936) – Warner Baxter & Gloria Stuart
Roar of the Press (1941) – Jean Parker & Wallace Ford
I Killed That Man (1941) – Ricardo Cortez
Shop at Sly Corner (1947) – Oscar Homolka & Muriel Pavlow
Personal Column (1939) – Maurice Chevalier & Marie Déa
Tarzan and the Huntress (1947) – Johnny Weissmuller & Brenda Joyce
Twin Husbands (1933) – John Miljan & Shirley Grey
Adventure Island (1947) – Rory Calhoun & Rhonda Fleming
Spring in Park Lane (1948) – Anna Neagle & Michael Wilding
Against the Wind (1948) – Jack Warner, Robert Beatty & Simone Signoret
The Noose Hangs High (1948) – Abbott & Costello
Miranda (1948) – Glynis Johns & Googie Withers
Sleeping Car to Trieste (1948) – Jean Kent & Albert Lieven
Killer McCoy (1947) – Mickey Rooney & Ann Blyth
The Invisible Man Returns (1940) – Cedric Hardwicke, Vincent Price & Nan Grey
Here Come the Huggetts (1948) – Jack Warner & Kathleen Harrison
Fame is the Spur (1947) – Michael Redgrave & Rosamund John
Odd Man Out (1947) – James Mason & Robert Newton
The Secret Life of Walter Mitty (1947) – Danny Kaye & Virginia Mayo
The Bride Goes Wild (1948) – Van Johnson & June Allyson
The Street with No Name (1948) – Mark Stevens & Barbara Lawrence
Easy Money (1948) – Greta Gynt, Dennis Price & Jack Warner
Take My Life (1947) – Hugh Williams & Greta Gynt
I See Ice (1938) – George Formby & Kay Walsh
Treasure of the Sierra Madre (1948) – Humphrey Bogart & Walter Huston
Out of the Blue (1947) – George Brent & Virginia Mayo
Things Happen at Night (1947) – Gordon Harker & Alfred Drayton
Call Northside 777 (1948) – James Stewart & Richard Conte
Portrait from Life (1948) – Mai Zetterling & Robert Beatty
For Them that Trespass (1949) – Stephen Murray & Patricia Plunkett
The Three Musketeers (1939) – Don Ameche & The Ritz Brothers
The Guinea Pig (1948) – Richard Attenborough & Sheila Sim